10 MINUTE GUIDE TO Quattro Pro® 6 for Windows™

Joe Kraynak

alpha books

A Division of Macmillan Computer Publishing
A Prentice Hall Macmillan Company
201 West 103rd Street, Indianapolis, Indiana 46290 USA

To Cecie Kraynak, an extraordinary woman who happens to be my wife.

©1994 by Alpha Books

All rights reserved. No part of this book shall be reproduced, stored in a retrieval system, or transmitted by any means, electronic, mechanical, photocopying, recording, or otherwise, without written permission from the publisher. No patent liability is assumed with respect to the use of the information contained herein. While every precaution has been taken in the preparation of this book, the publisher and author assume no responsibility for errors or omissions. Neither is any liability assumed for damages resulting from the use of the information contained herein. For more information, write to Alpha Books, 210 West 103rd Street, Indianapolis, IN 46290.

International Standard Book Number: 1-56761-536-8
Library of Congress Catalog Card Number: 94-78722

97 96 95 94   8 7 6 5 4 3 2 1

Interpretation of the printing code: the rightmost double-digit number is the year of the book's first printing; the rightmost single-digit number is the number of the book's printing. For example, a printing code of 94-1 shows that the first printing of the book was in 1994.

Screen reproductions in this book were created by means of the program Collage Plus from Inner Media, Inc., Hollis, NH.

Printed in the United States of America

Publisher: *Marie Butler-Knight*
Managing Editor: *Elizabeth Keaffaber*
Product Development Manager: *Faithe Wempen*
Acquisitions Manager: *Barry Pruett*
Development Editor: *Heather Stith*
Technical Editor: *Herbert Feltner*
Production Editor: *Kelly Oliver*
Manuscript Editor: *Barry Childs-Helton*
Cover Design: *Dan Armstrong*
Indexer: *Chris Cleveland*
Production: *Dan Caparo, Brad Chinn, Kim Cofer, Lisa Daugherty, David Dean, Jennifer Eberhardt, David Garratt, Erika Millen, Beth Rago, Bobbi Satterfield, Karen Walsh, Robert Wolf*

Contents

1 Starting and Exiting Quattro Pro, 1

Starting Quattro Pro, 1
Getting Help, 2
Exiting Quattro Pro, 4

2 Moving Around in the Quattro Pro Window, 5

Navigating the Quattro Pro Window, 5
Navigating the Notebook Window, 6

3 Entering Labels, Values, and Dates, 11

Understanding Labels and Values, 11
Entering Data, 12
Aligning an Entry in a Cell, 15
Entering Data Quickly with SpeedFill, 16

4 Entering Formulas, 18

Understanding Formulas, 18
Understanding the Order of Operations, 19
Entering Formulas, 20
Copying Formulas, 21
Using Absolute Cell References, 21
Changing the Recalculation Setting, 22

5 Entering Functions, 24

Understanding Functions, 24
Using SpeedSum, 24
Entering Functions with the Formula Composer, 25
Using Logical Operators, 27

6 Saving, Closing, and Opening Notebooks, 30

Saving Spreadsheet Notebooks, 30
Closing a Notebook, 33
Opening a Notebook, 33
Making a New Notebook, 34
Switching Notebook Windows, 35

7 Selecting and Naming Cells, 36

Selecting Multiple Cells, 36
Specifying Blocks in Dialog Boxes, 38
Using Named Cells and Ranges, 39

8 Editing Cells, 42

Editing the Contents of a Cell, 42
Undoing Changes, 43
Deleting Cell Contents, 44
Copying and Moving Cells
  with Drag and Drop, 44
Copying and Cutting Cells
  to the Clipboard, 46
Pasting Cells from the Clipboard, 46
Copying and Moving Cell Blocks, 47

9 Controlling Columns and Rows, 48

Changing the Column Width, 48
Changing the Row Height, 50
Inserting Rows, Columns, or Blocks, 51
Deleting a Row or Column, 52
Locking Column and Row Titles, 53

10 Enhancing the Appearance of Labels and Values, 55

Formatting Values, 55
Changing Fonts, 57
Aligning Text in Cells, 58

11 Adding Lines and Shading to Cells and Blocks, 61

Drawing Lines Around and Between Cells, 61
Hiding the Grid Lines, 63
Shading a Cell or Cell Block, 63

12 Formatting with SpeedFormat and Styles, 65

Quick Formatting with SpeedFormat, 65
Understanding Styles, 66
Applying Existing Styles, 67
Creating Custom Styles, 68
Changing Styles, 69

13 Setting Up a Page for Printing, 70

Setting Up a Page, 70
Selecting a Paper Type and Orientation, 71
Adding a Header and Footer, 72
Setting the Margins, 73
Scaling Your Spreadsheet, 74

14 Printing Your Spreadsheet, 76

Quick Printing, 76
Previewing Your Printout, 77
Selecting Special Print Options, 79

15 Working with Notebook Pages, 82

Working with Notebook Pages, 82
Naming Notebook Pages, 82
Changing Notebook Page Settings, 83
Working with Groups of Pages, 84
Drilling Entries on Groups of Pages, 86

16 Creating Graphs, 87

Understanding Quattro Pro's Graph Types and Terminology, 87
Using the Graph Expert, 88

Moving and Resizing a Graph, 90
Modifying a Graph, 91

17 Enhancing and Printing Graphs, 93

Displaying a Graph in the Edit Window, 93
Customizing a Graph with Object Inspectors, 94
Adding Graphic Objects, 96
Printing a Graph, 99

18 Creating a Slide Show, 100

What Is a Slide Show?, 100
Creating a Bullet Chart, 100
Creating a Slide Show, 102
Using the Slide Show Expert, 103
Customizing Your Slide Show, 104
Printing a Slide Show, 105

19 Creating a Database, 107

Understanding Database Basics, 107
Creating a Database, 108
Adding Records, 109
Saving the Database, 110

20 Sorting and Searching a Database, 111

Sorting a Database, 111
Searching for Records, 113

21 Using the Home Finance Tools, 119

Using the Budget Expert, 119
Refinancing a Loan, 122
Creating an Amortization Schedule, 125

22 Analyzing Data with Data Models, 128

Opening a New Report, 129
Building a Crosstab Report, 131
Rearranging Your Data, 132
Creating Totals, 133
Using the Data Modeling Gadgets, 133
Changing the Font Size, 134
Copying the Report to a Notebook, 134

23 Using Scenarios to Predict Results, 135

What Are Scenarios?, 135
Creating Scenarios with Scenario Expert, 136
Using the Scenario Manager, 138

24 Automating Your Work with Macros, 141

What Is a Macro?, 141
Recording a Macro, 141
Playing Back a Macro, 143
Making a Macro Library, 144

Microsoft Windows Primer, 146

Starting Microsoft Windows, 146
Parts of a Windows Screen, 147
Using a Mouse, 148
Starting an Application, 150
Using Menus, 150
Navigating Dialog Boxes, 151
Right-Clicking in Quattro Pro, 153

Index, 155

Introduction

Perhaps you walked into work this morning and found Quattro Pro for Windows on your desk. A note is stuck to the box: "We need a budget for the upcoming meeting. See what you can do."

Now what? You could wade through the manuals that came with the program to find out how to perform a specific task, but that may take a while, and it may tell you more than you want to know. You need a practical guide, one that will tell you exactly how to create and print a spreadsheet for the meeting.

Welcome to the *10 Minute Guide to Quattro Pro 6 for Windows*

Because most people don't have the luxury of sitting down uninterrupted for hours at a time to learn Quattro Pro, this *10 Minute Guide* does not attempt to teach *everything* about the program. Instead, it focuses on the most often-used features. Each feature is covered in a single self-contained lesson, which is designed to take 10 minutes or less to complete.

This *10 Minute Guide* teaches you about Quattro Pro without relying on technical jargon. With straightforward, easy-to-follow explanations and numbered lists that tell you which keys to press and which options to select, the *10 Minute Guide to Quattro Pro 6 for Windows* makes learning Quattro Pro quick and easy.

Introduction   ix

Who Should Use the *10 Minute Guide to Quattro Pro 6 for Windows*?

The *10 Minute Guide to Quattro Pro 6 for Windows* is for anyone who

- Needs to learn Quattro Pro for Windows quickly.
- Feels overwhelmed or intimidated by the complexity of Quattro Pro.
- Wants to find out quickly whether Quattro Pro for Windows will meet his or her spreadsheet needs.
- Wants a clear, concise guide to the most important features of Quattro Pro for Windows.

What Is Quattro Pro for Windows?

Quattro Pro for Windows is an innovative spreadsheet program designed specifically for the Windows operating environment. Using a familiar row-and-column format, Quattro Pro allows you to manipulate data in a variety of ways. Instead of using ledger paper, a calculator, and a pencil, you can use Quattro Pro to do both simple and complex number-crunching activities.

Quattro Pro represents a fresh approach to spreadsheets, providing several features you won't find in any other spreadsheet program. These features include the following:

- *Object inspectors.* With a click of the right mouse button, you are presented with a menu that allows you to change the properties of the currently selected object.
- *Toolbars.* Toolbars contain a collection of icons that allow you to access the most commonly used features with the click of a button.

- *3-D spreadsheet notebooks.* This notebook approach lets you create a three-dimensional spreadsheet consisting of up to 256 spreadsheet pages. Tabs provide a convenient way to flip pages.

- *Graphing and slide show tools.* Quattro Pro can quickly convert your data into graphs or bullet charts. You can then transform your graphs and charts into an on-screen slide-show, or you can print them out.

- *Home-finance Experts.* Quattro Pro comes with several Experts that can lead you through the process of creating budget, refinance, and loan amortization spreadsheets.

How to Use This Book

The *10 Minute Guide to Quattro Pro 6 for Windows* consists of a series of lessons, ranging from basic startup to a few more advanced features. If this is your first encounter with Quattro Pro for Windows, you should probably work through lessons 1 to 15 in order. These lessons lead you through the process of creating, editing, and printing a spreadsheet. Subsequent lessons tell you how to use the more advanced features; these include using your spreadsheet as a database, as well as creating, enhancing, and printing graphs.

If Quattro Pro for Windows has not been installed on your computer, consult the inside front cover for installation steps. If this is your first encounter with Microsoft Windows, turn to the Windows Primer at the end of this book for help.

Icons and Conventions Used in This Book

The following icons have been added throughout the book to help you find your way around:

Timesaver Tip icons offer shortcuts and hints for using the program efficiently.

Plain English icons define new terms.

Panic Button icons appear where new users often run into trouble.

The following conventions have been used to clarify the steps you must perform:

On-screen text	Any text that appears on-screen appears in bold type.
What you type	The information you type appears in bold color type.
Press Enter	Keys you press (or selections you make with the mouse) appear in color type.
Key+Key Combinations	In many cases, you must press a two-key key combination in order to enter a command. For example, "Press Alt+X." In such cases, hold down the first key while pressing the second key.

Trademarks

All terms mentioned in this book that are known to be trademarks or service marks are listed below. In addition, terms suspected of being trademarks or service marks have been appropriately capitalized. Alpha Books cannot attest to the accuracy of this information. Use of a term in this book should not be regarded as affecting the validity of any trademark or service mark.

Quattro Pro is a registered trademark of Borland International, Inc.

MS-DOS is a registered trademark of Microsoft Corporation.

Microsoft Windows is a registered trademark of Microsoft Corporation.

Lesson 1

Starting and Exiting Quattro Pro

In this lesson, you'll learn how to start and end a typical Quattro Pro work session, and how to get online help.

Starting Quattro Pro

After you install Quattro Pro, the installation program returns you to the Program Manager and displays the Quattro Pro for Windows program group window (as shown in Figure 1.1). To start Quattro Pro, double-click on the Quattro Pro for Windows program-item icon. The Welcome to Quattro Pro dialog box appears, allowing you to run Coaches (a help-feature) or run Quattro Pro. Click on the Quattro Pro button.

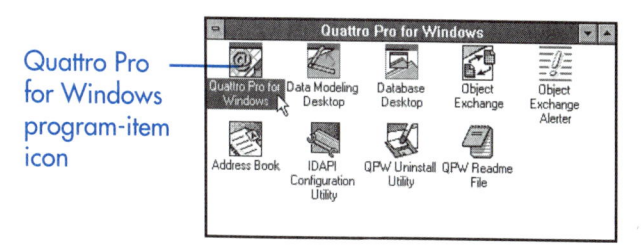

Figure 1.1 Double-click on the Quattro Pro for Windows program-item icon.

The Quattro Pro opening screen appears (see Figure 1.2) with a blank spreadsheet notebook labeled NOTEBK1.WB2. Quattro Pro is now ready for you to begin creating your spreadsheet notebook.

Lesson 1

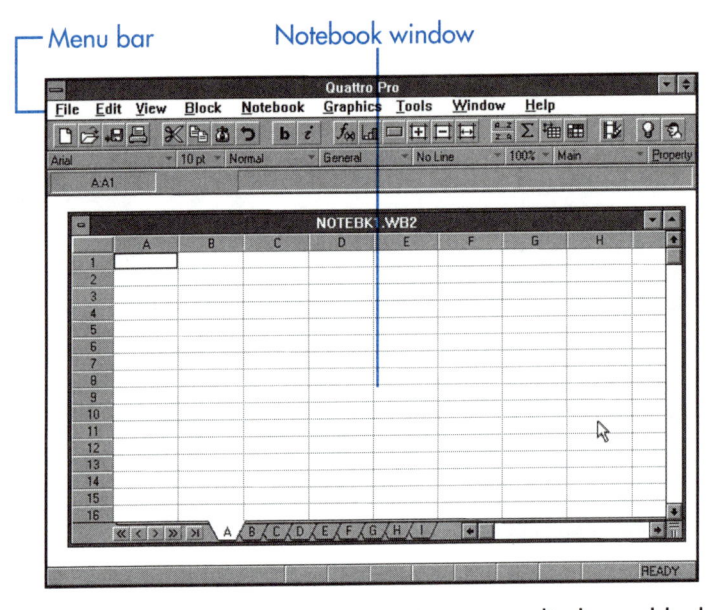

Figure 1.2 Quattro Pro's opening screen displays a blank spreadsheet notebook.

Spreadsheet Notebook Quattro Pro files are called *notebooks*. Each notebook consists of 256 spreadsheet pages, plus one page for graphs. Each spreadsheet page consists of columns and rows that intersect to form boxes called *cells*.

Getting Help

The following list explains the various ways you can get help in Quattro Pro:

- **Open the Help menu and select a command.**
  The Help menu offers the following options:

Starting and Exiting Quattro Pro   3

Contents displays a list of Help topics. Click on the desired topic.

Search helps you find specific help. Start typing the name of the task or command for which you need help, until the topic appears in the list. Double-click on the topic to display a list of subtopics. Double-click on the desired subtopic.

Experts lead you through the process of using special spreadsheet features. For example, an Expert can help you construct a budget for tracking home expenses.

Coaches lead you through the process of using basic commands and spreadsheet features. When you select a Coach Help topic, a dialog box appears, displaying step-by-step instructions on how to perform the selected task.

About Quattro Pro displays general information about Quattro Pro and the amount of memory available on your computer.

- **Press F1.** If you highlight a command or display a dialog box before pressing F1, Quattro Pro displays information about that command or dialog box. If you do not highlight a command or open a dialog box, Quattro Pro displays a list of Help topics.

- **Move the mouse pointer over a Toolbar button.** This displays the name of the Toolbar button.

- **Ctrl+right-click on an object to display Object Help.** To display a brief description of an object (for example, a Toolbar button, a page tab, or a cell), move the mouse pointer over the object, then hold down the Ctrl key and the right mouse button.

Most help screens contain *jumps*, which are highlighted terms that provide quick links to related topics. If you click on a jump that is underlined with a solid line, Quattro Pro displays a Help screen with information about that topic. If you click on a jump that is underlined with a dotted line, Quattro Pro displays a definition for the selected term.

To exit the Help screen, press Esc or double-click on the Control-menu box in the upper left corner of the Help window.

Exiting Quattro Pro

To exit Quattro Pro and return to Windows, follow these steps:

1. Click on File in the menu bar.

2. Click on Exit.

If you changed the spreadsheet in any way without saving the file, Quattro Pro will display a prompt asking whether you want to save the file before exiting. Select the desired option.

> **Quick Exit** For a quick exit, press Alt+F4 or double-click on the Control-menu box in the upper left corner of the Quattro Pro window.

In this lesson, you learned how to start and quit Quattro Pro, and how to get online help. In the next lesson, you'll learn how to move around in the Quattro Pro notebook window.

Lesson 2

Moving Around in the Quattro Pro Window

In this lesson, you'll learn the basics of moving around in the Quattro Pro window and the notebook window.

Navigating the Quattro Pro Window

As you can see in Figure 2.1, the Quattro Pro window contains several elements that allow you to enter commands and data:

Menu bar Displays the names of the available *pull-down menus*. When you select a menu, it drops down over a portion of the screen, presenting you with a list of options.

Toolbar Contains buttons that enable you to bypass the menu commands.

Property Band Contains pull-down lists for changing the *format* (appearance) of your entries.

Input line Displays an entry as you type it. When you press Enter, the information is inserted in the selected cell.

Notebook window Contains the notebook, where you enter the data and formulas that make up your spreadsheet.

Status line Displays information about the current activity, including Help information and keyboard and program modes.

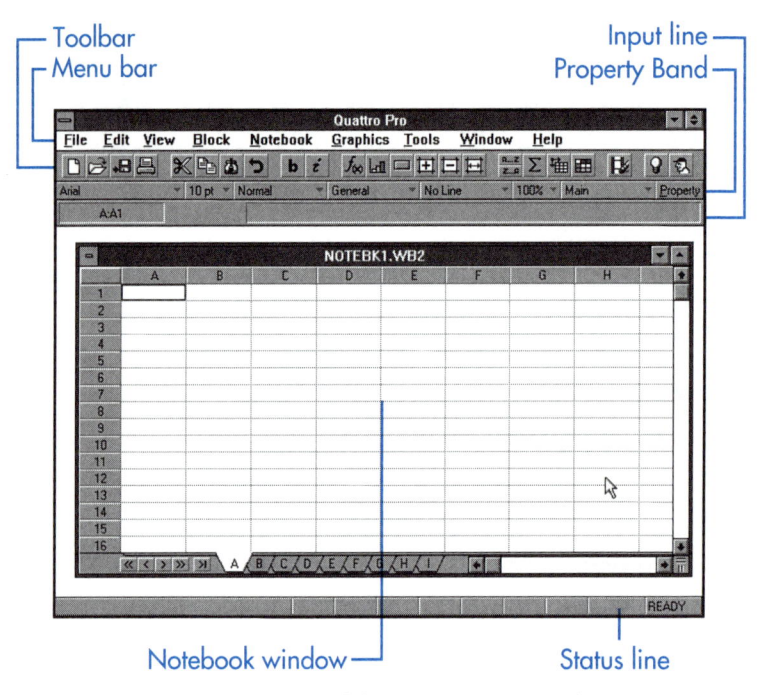

Figure 2.1 Elements of the Quattro Pro window.

Navigating the Notebook Window

Inside the Quattro Pro window is a notebook window. In this window, you enter the labels, values, and formulas that make up your spreadsheet. As shown in Figure 2.2, the notebook window consists of the following parts:

Tabs enable you to turn notebook pages. A notebook consists of 256 spreadsheet pages, plus one page for graphs.

Moving Around in the Quattro Pro Window 7

Tab scroll controls allow you to flip quickly through the pages in the notebook.

SpeedTab button goes to the last or first notebook page. On the first notebook page, the arrow points to the right. On the last page, it points to the left.

Scroll bars allow you to view a section of the current spreadsheet page that is not displayed.

Column border identifies the columns by letters.

Row border identifies the rows by numbers.

Select-All button selects all the cells on the page.

Selector indicates the selected cell or cells.

Pane splitter lets you split the notebook window into two panes to view different portions of the same spreadsheet page.

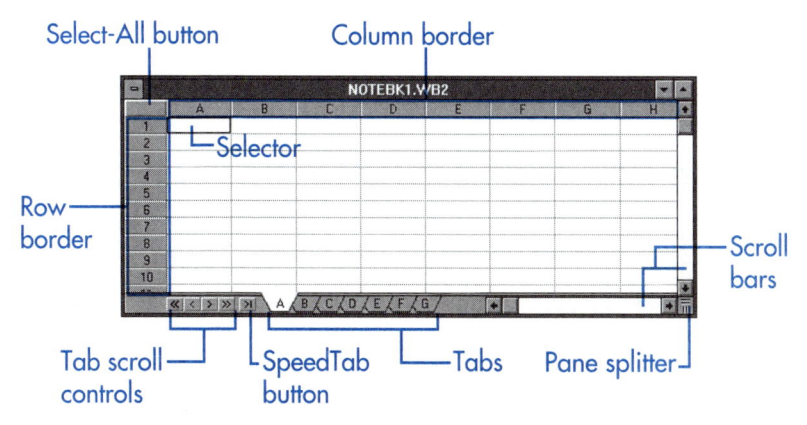

Figure 2.2 Elements of the notebook window.

Lesson 2

Cell Each page in a notebook is a separate spreadsheet. Each spreadsheet contains a grid consisting of alphabetized columns and numbered rows. When a row and column intersect, they form a box called a *cell*. You enter data and formulas into the cells to form a spreadsheet.

Plain English

Flipping Notebook Pages

Because each notebook consists of 256 pages, you need a way to move from page to page. With the keyboard, you can flip pages by pressing Ctrl+PgDn and Ctrl+PgUp. With a mouse, you can flip to a page by clicking on its tab. If you can't see the desired tab, use the tab scroll controls, as shown in Figure 2.3.

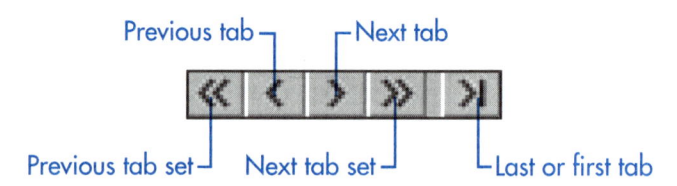

Figure 2.3 Use the tab scroll controls to flip notebook pages.

Moving Around on a Spreadsheet Page

Once the page you want to work on is displayed, you need some way of moving to the various cells on the page. To move around the page with your keyboard, use the keys as described in Table 2.1.

Table 2.1 Moving the Selector with the Keyboard

Press	To move
← ← ↑ ↓	One cell in the direction of the arrow.
Ctrl+→	Right one screen.

Moving Around in the Quattro Pro Window   9

Press	To move
Ctrl+←	Left one screen.
PgUp	Up one screen.
PgDn	Down one screen.
Home	To the upper left cell on current page.
Ctrl+Home	To the upper left cell on first page.
End+Home	To the last non-blank cell on the page.
Ctrl+End+Home	To the last non-blank cell in the notebook.
End+↑, End+↓, End+←, End+→	If the active cell is blank, moves to the next blank cell in the direction of the arrow. If the active cell contains an entry, moves in the direction of the arrow to the next cell that has an entry.

If you have a mouse, moving on a page is easier. Use the scroll bars to scroll to the area of the screen that contains the cell you want to work with, then click on the cell. The following figure shows how to use the scroll bars.

Click on a scroll arrow at the end of the scroll bar to scroll incrementally in the direction of the arrow. Hold down the mouse button to scroll continuously.

Drag the scroll box inside the scroll bar to the area of the page you want to view. For example, to move to the middle of the page, drag the scroll box to the middle of the scroll bar.

Click inside the scroll bar, on either side of the scroll box, to move the view one screen at a time.

Quick Moves To move to a specific cell on a page, pull down the *Edit* menu and select *Go to*, or press *F5*. Type the column letter and row number of the desired cell (for example, **M25**), and click on the *OK* button. To go to a cell on another page in the notebook, precede the column letter and row number with the page letter and a colon (for example, **D:M25**).

Splitting a Spreadsheet Page

Because a spreadsheet page can be so large, you may want to view different parts of the spreadsheet at the same time. To do this, you need to split the notebook window into *panes*. To split a notebook window, take the following steps:

1. Move the mouse pointer over the *pane splitter* (see Figure 2.2). To split the window horizontally, move the pointer over the top half of the tool. To split vertically, use the bottom half.

2. Hold down the mouse button and drag the pointer to where you want the window split. A line appears, showing where Quattro Pro will split the window.

3. Release the mouse button. Quattro Pro splits the window.

4. To switch from one pane to the other, click in the pane you want to work with, or press *F6*.

To close a pane, drag the pane splitter on the top (or left) pane to the bottom (or right) edge of the notebook window.

In this lesson, you learned how to move around in the Quattro Pro window and notebooks. In the next lesson, you will learn how to enter data into notebook pages.

Lesson 3

Entering Labels, Values, and Dates

In this lesson, you'll learn how to enter data into a notebook.

Understanding Labels and Values

Every spreadsheet consists of three types of entries: labels, values (and dates), and formulas. *Labels* consist of text entries, such as entries you would use for column and row headings. *Values* consist of numeric entries. *Formulas* are entries which perform mathematical operations on the values you enter. Figure 3.1 illustrates how the various spreadsheet entries interact.

Labels describe the contents of the cells.

Values

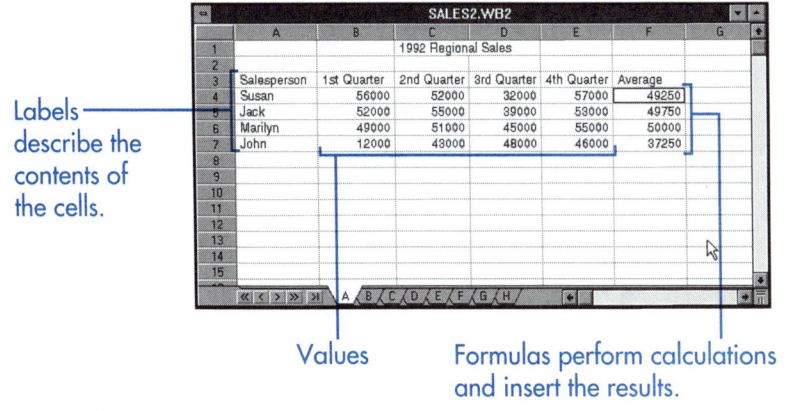

Formulas perform calculations and insert the results.

Figure 3.1 A typical spreadsheet contains labels, values, and formulas.

Lesson 3

In this lesson, you will learn how to enter labels, values, and dates. In Lesson 4, you will learn how to enter formulas.

Entering Data

Except for some special circumstances, entering data into a spreadsheet is a very simple operation. Here's what you do:

1. Move the selector to the cell in which you want the data to appear. (Either click inside the cell or use the arrow keys to move the selector.)

2. Type one of the following entries:

> **Label:** Type the text you want to use for the label. You cannot use the following characters:
> / + - $ (@ . # =
>
> **Value:** Type a numerical entry. Do not type a dollar sign, percent sign, or any other symbol. (Lesson 10 explains the correct way to add these symbols.)
>
> **Date:** Type a date in the form MM/DD/YY.

The text appears on the *input line*, as shown in Figure 3.2.

Click here to cancel. — Click here to confirm.

[@ { } X ✓ | Salesperson]

As you type, the entry appears here.

Figure 3.2 Whatever you type appears first on the input line.

3. To edit your entry, backspace over incorrect characters and type your corrections.

Entering Labels, Values, and Dates

4. Click on the check mark to the left of the input line, or press Enter. This transfers the entry from the input line into the selected cell. (To cancel an entry, click on the X to the left of the input line, or press Esc.)

> **Enter and Move On** After typing your entry, press → or ↓ to enter the label into the cell and move the selector to the next cell.

Using Insert and Overtype

By default, when you type text on the input line, whatever you type is inserted at the insertion point. Any existing text is shifted to the right to accommodate the new text. If you want to type over existing text rather than insert text, you can switch to Overtype mode. To switch modes, press the Ins (Insert) key. When you are in Overtype mode, you'll see **OVR** on the right side of the status line. To switch back to Insert mode, press the Ins key again.

Entering Numbers as a Label

If you type any of the following characters as the first character in a label, Quattro Pro will treat the label as a value or formula instead of as a label:

0 1 2 3 4 5 6 7 8 9 + - . (@ # $

To trick Quattro Pro into treating the numerical entry as a label, precede the entry with one of the alignment characters described in the section "Aligning an Entry in a Cell." For example, type **'555-1212** to have Quattro Pro treat the phone number as a label instead of as an equation (555 minus 1212). This trick also comes in handy when you're entering ZIP codes.

Lesson 3

> **Label Your Numbers** Another way to make Quattro Pro treat numerical entries as labels is to drag over the desired cells, then right-click on one of the selected cells. Click on Block Properties, click on Constraints, and click on Labels Only. Click on OK. In the selected cells, all entries will now be treated as labels. For details on how to select cells, refer to Lesson 7.

Handling Long Entries

If you type a label that's wider than the cell, the label will overlap any empty cells to the right of the current cell. If the cell to the right is not empty, Quattro Pro will display as much of the label as possible in the current cell, as shown in Figure 3.3. To widen the column and display the entire entry, skip ahead to Lesson 9.

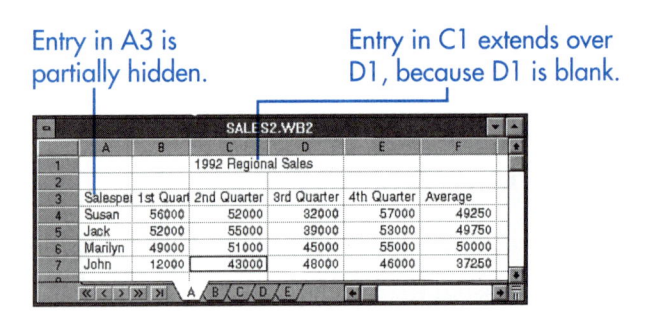

Entry in A3 is partially hidden.

Entry in C1 extends over D1, because D1 is blank.

	A	B	C	D	E	F
1			1992 Regional Sales			
2						
3	Salespe	1st Quart	2nd Quarter	3rd Quarter	4th Quarter	Average
4	Susan	56000	52000	32000	57000	49250
5	Jack	52000	55000	39000	53000	49750
6	Marilyn	49000	51000	45000	55000	50000
7	John	12000	43000	48000	46000	37250

Figure 3.3 Quattro Pro lets labels overlap cells if the cells are empty; otherwise you see only a portion of the entry.

Entering Dates

You can type a date in various ways, depending on how you want the date to appear in your spreadsheet. Table 3.1 lists the available date formats.

Table 3.1 Date Formats

Date Format	Example
DD-MMM-YY	04-Feb-94
DD-MMM	04-Feb (of the current year)
MMM-YY	Feb-94 (first day of the month)
MM/DD/YY	02/04/94
MM/DD	02/04 (of the current year)

Quattro Pro displays the date as you typed it, but if you select the cell that contains the date entry, the input line displays the number of days that have passed since December 30, 1899. Quattro Pro uses this number in date calculations. For example, you can use a date calculation to determine whether a payment is past due.

Aligning an Entry in a Cell

When you enter a label into a cell, Quattro Pro left-aligns the label in the cell. To select an alignment as you enter the label, type one of the following characters before typing the label:

- '   Left-aligns the text.
- ^   Centers the text.
- "   Right-aligns the text.

To change the alignment of an existing entry, right-click on the cell and select Block Properties from the menu that appears. A dialog box appears. Select Alignment in the left column of the dialog box to display the alignment options in the right column. Select the alignment option you want, and click on the OK button.

Aligning Dates and Values Do not type an alignment character in front of a value or date. If you do, Quattro Pro will treat the number as a label. To change the alignment of a value or date, right-click on the cell, choose Block Properties, and then choose the desired alignment.

Entering Data Quickly with SpeedFill

Quattro Pro offers a feature called SpeedFill, which inserts a series of entries based on a single *seed* entry. For example, to enter the days of the week (Sunday through Saturday), you type the first entry (Sunday), and SpeedFill inserts the other entries for you. Try it:

1. Type **Monday** into a cell and press Enter.

2. Move the mouse pointer over the cell that contains **Monday**, hold down the mouse button, and drag over six more cells down or to the right.

3. Click on the SpeedFill button. Quattro Pro inserts the remaining days of the week, in order, into the selected cells.

   Quattro Pro has several SpeedFill series. To check them out, click on an empty cell. Then click on the SpeedFill button on the Toolbar to display the SpeedFill dialog box. All the series are listed in the Series Name drop-down list, and their elements are listed in the Series Elements list box. If none of the series meets your needs, you can create your own custom series by performing the following steps:

1. From the SpeedFill dialog box, click on Create. The Create Series dialog box appears.

2. Type a description of the new series in the Series Name text box.

Entering Labels, Values, and Dates

3. In the Series Type area, click on List, and (optional) click on Repeating if you want the series to repeat.

4. Click in the Value text box, and type an item you want to appear in the series.

5. Click on the Add button.

6. Repeat steps 4 and 5 to add more items to the series. (SpeedFill inserts items in the order in which you type them.)

7. Click on the OK button.

8. Click on the OK button to return to the notebook.

Extracting a Series from the Spreadsheet If you already typed the series in a range of cells, you can copy that series instead of retyping it in the Create Series dialog box. Click on the Extract button, drag over the cells that contain the series, and then click on OK.

In this lesson, you learned how to enter labels, values, and dates into cells, and how to use the SpeedFill tool. In the next lesson, you will learn how to enter formulas to perform calculations on your values.

Lesson 4

Entering Formulas

In this lesson, you'll learn how to enter formulas to perform mathematical operations on values.

Understanding Formulas

Spreadsheets use *formulas* to perform calculations on the data you enter. With formulas, you can perform addition, subtraction, multiplication, or division using the values contained in various cells. Figure 4.1 shows several formulas in action.

+E4+E5+E6 gives total income for the 4th Quarter.

	A	B	C	D	E	F	G
1	Hokey Manufacturing						
2							
3	Income	1st Qtr	2nd Qtr	3rd Qtr	4th Qtr		
4	Wholesale	55000	46000	52000	90900		
5	Retail	45700	56500	42800	57900		
6	Special	23000	54800	67000	45800		
7	Total	123700	157300	161800	194600		
8							
9	Expenses						
10	Materials	19000	17500	18200	20500		
11	Labor	15000	15053	15500	15400		
12	Rent	1600	1600	1600	1600		
13	Misc.	2500	2550	3000	1500		
14	Total	38100	36703	38300	39000		
15						Total Profit	
16	Profit	85600	120597	123500	155600	485297	
17							

+E10+E11+E12+E13 gives total expenses for the 4th Quarter.

+B16+C16+D16+E16 totals the four Quarter profits to determine total profit.

+E7−E14 subtracts expenses from income to determine profit.

Figure 4.1 Type a formula in the cell where you want the resulting value to appear.

Entering Formulas

Formulas typically consist of one or more *cell addresses* and/or values and a mathematical operator, such as + (addition), − (subtraction), * (multiplication), or / (division). For example, to determine the average of the three values contained in cells A1, B1, and C1, you would use the following formula:

(A1+B1+C1)/3

> **Cell Address** A cell address is a coordinate made up of the cell's column letter and row number. The cell address specifies the location of data in the spreadsheet.

Every formula must begin with one of the following characters:

0 1 2 3 4 5 6 7 8 9 . + − @ # $ (

Understanding the Order of Operations

Quattro Pro performs a series of operations from left to right, giving some operators *precedence* over others. Multiplication and division are performed first. Addition and subtraction are performed second.

This order is important to keep in mind when you are creating equations, because the order of operations determines the result. For example, if you want to determine the average of the values in cells A1, B1, and C1, and you enter +A1+B1+C1/3, you'll get the wrong answer. The value in C1 will be divided by 3, and that result will be added to A1+B1. To determine the total of A1 through C1 first, you must enclose that group of values in parentheses: **(A1+B1+C1)/3**.

My Dear Aunt Sally Use this mnemonic device to remember the order of operations: **M**y **D**ear **A**unt **S**ally (**M**ultiplication, **D**ivision, **A**ddition, **S**ubtraction).

Entering Formulas

You can enter formulas in either of two ways: by *typing* the formula or by *pointing*. If you choose to type the formula, be sure to start with a plus sign (+) or other appropriate character, as explained earlier. Pointing allows you to enter the cell addresses by clicking on the cells you want to use in the formula. Here's what you do:

1. Click inside the cell in which you want the formula to appear.

2. Type + or any of the characters required to start the formula.

3. Click on the cell whose address you want to appear first in the formula. The cell address appears on the input line.

4. Type a mathematical operator after the value to indicate the next operation you want to perform. The operator appears on the input line.

5. Continue clicking on cells and typing operators (and/or values) until the formula is complete.

6. Press Enter to accept the formula, or Esc to cancel the operation.

Copying Formulas

To use the same formula in several cells, you can save time by copying the formula. Quattro Pro adjusts the cell references in the formulas relative to their new positions in the worksheet. For example, in Figure 4.1, cell B7 contains the formula +B4+B5+B6, which determines the total 1st Quarter income. If you copy that formula to cell C7 (to determine the total 2nd Quarter income), Quattro Pro automatically changes the formula to +C4+C5+C6. For more information on copying cell contents, see Lesson 8.

> **Relative and Absolute References**
> Normally, Quattro Pro treats cell addresses in a formula as *relative references*, and changes the addresses if you move or copy the formula. You can mark addresses as *absolute references* (see the next section), to prevent Quattro Pro from adjusting them.

Using Absolute Cell References

Suppose you want to copy a formula that refers to the same cell in every case. For example, in Figure 4.2, cell C11 contains a formula which multiplies the sales figure in C9 by the overhead percentage in cell C3 to determine the overhead expense. If you were to copy the formula in cell C11 into cell D11, the formula would be +D9*D3, but because there is no entry in cell D3, it would result in an error message. To have each copy of the formula refer to cell C3, you must mark the C3 cell reference as an absolute reference.

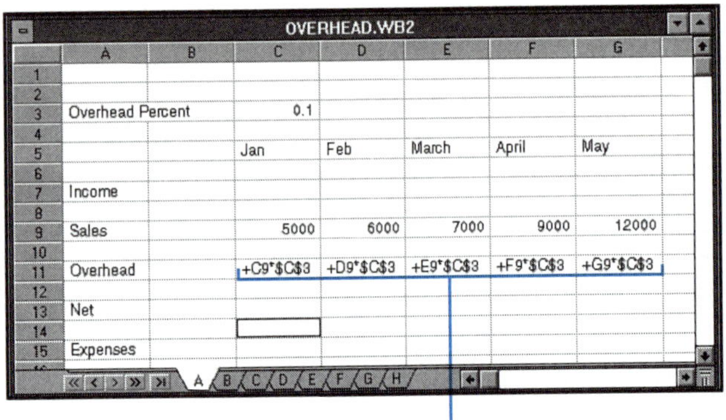

Lesson 4

	A	B	C	D	E	F	G
1							
2							
3	Overhead Percent		0.1				
4							
5			Jan	Feb	March	April	May
6							
7	Income						
8							
9	Sales		5000	6000	7000	9000	12000
10							
11	Overhead		+C9*C3	+D9*C3	+E9*C3	+F9*C3	+G9*C3
12							
13	Net						
14							
15	Expenses						

Absolute references remain fixed when copied to another cell.

Figure 4.2 Absolute references do not change when copied. (Formulas do not normally appear in cells; this figure is an illustration.)

To make a cell reference absolute, you add a $ (dollar sign) to the cell address. You can either type the dollar sign(s) on the input line, or follow these steps to mark an absolute reference:

1. Click on the cell that contains the formula. The formula appears on the input line.

2. In the input line, highlight the cell address you want to make absolute.

3. Press F4, the Absolute Value key. Pressing it once makes the page letter, column letter, and row number of the cell reference absolute. You can press F4 repeatedly to turn off the absolute reference for the page, column, and/or row.

Changing the Recalculation Setting

Quattro Pro recalculates the formulas in a worksheet every time you edit a value in a cell. However, on a large worksheet, you may not want Quattro Pro to recalculate until you have entered all your changes. To change the recalculation setting, take the following steps:

1. Right-click on the notebook window's title bar.

2. Select Recalc Settings. The recalculation settings appear, as shown in Figure 4.3.

3. In the Mode group, select one of the following options:

    Automatic automatically recalculates all affected formulas.

    Manual recalculates affected formulas when you press F9.

    Background recalculates all affected formulas between keystrokes; you can continue working while Quattro Pro is recalculating.

4. Click on the OK button.

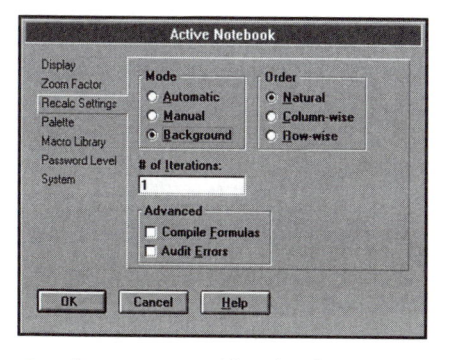

Figure 4.3 The Active Notebook Object Inspector lets you change the recalculation settings.

In this lesson, you learned how to construct formulas by using cell references and mathematical operators. In the next lesson, you will learn how to use Quattro Pro's built-in functions and the SpeedSum feature.

Lesson 5

Entering Functions

In this lesson, you'll learn how to enter functions and use the Formula Composer and the SpeedSum feature.

Understanding Functions

Functions are complex, ready-made formulas that perform a series of operations on a specified *range* of values. For example, to determine the sum of a series of numbers in cells A1 through H1, you can enter the function @SUM(A1..H1), instead of entering +A1+B1+C1+ and so on. Every function consists of the following three elements:

- The @ sign indicates that what follows is a function.
- The *function name* (for example, SUM) indicates the operation that will be performed.
- The *argument*, for example (A1..H1), indicates the cell addresses of the values that the function will act on. The argument is often a range of cells, but it can be much more complex.

Using SpeedSum

Because adding a row or column of numbers is the most common operation you'll perform in spreadsheets, Quattro Pro offers a SpeedSum feature which inserts the @SUM function for you. To use the feature, take the following steps:

1. Drag the mouse pointer over the row or column of numbers you want to total, and over one blank cell, as shown in Figure 5.1. (You must select one blank cell to indicate where you want the sum placed.)

2. Click on the SpeedSum button. Quattro Pro totals the values in the selected cells and inserts the sum into the blank cell.

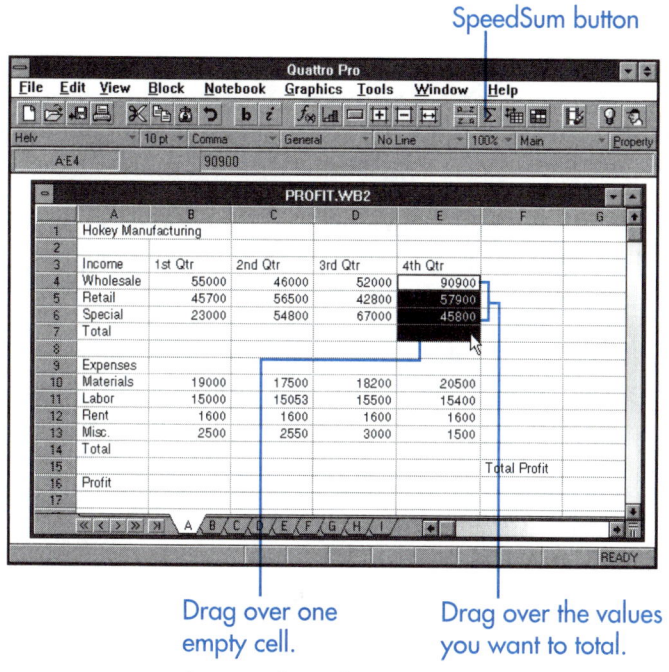

Figure 5.1 The SpeedSum feature lets you total a column or row of values quickly.

Entering Functions with the Formula Composer

Although you can type a function and argument, just as you can type formulas, Quattro Pro offers an easier way to enter functions: the Formula Composer. Take the following steps:

Lesson 5

1. Select the cell in which you want to insert the function. (You can insert a function by itself or as part of a formula.)

2. Click on the Formula Composer button. The Formula Expert dialog box appears.

3. Click on the @ button to view a list of functions.

4. In the Function Category list, click on the type of function you want to insert. Quattro Pro displays the names of the available functions in the function list.

5. From the Function list, click on the function you want to insert. A brief description of the function appears at the bottom of the dialog box.

6. Click on the OK button. You return to the Formula Expert dialog box, which provides additional details about the function (see Figure 5.2). In the lower right section of the dialog box is a list of the items that comprise the argument. You must enter a cell address or value for each item.

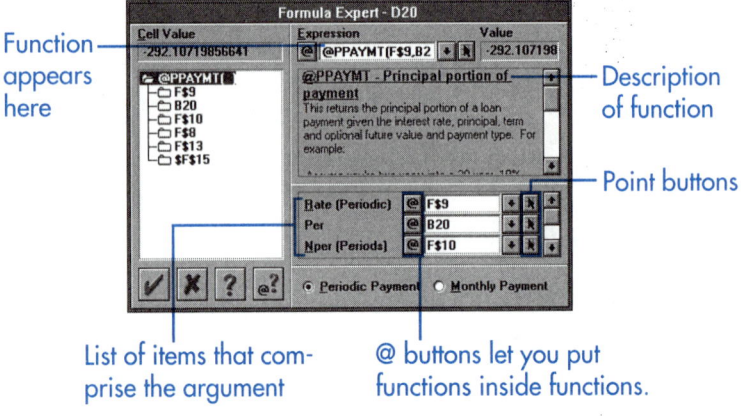

Figure 5.2 Use the Formula Composer to enter functions quickly.

Entering Functions 27

7. Click on an item in the argument list (start with the first item).

8. Perform one of the following steps:

    To add a cell address to the argument, click on the Point button to the right of the item. When you click on the Point button, the Formula Expert dialog box disappears except for the title bar, and you are returned to the notebook window. Click the cell or cells you want, then click on the Maximize button in the Formula Expert title bar to display the dialog box.

    To add a value to the argument, type the value inside the text box.

9. Repeat steps 7 and 8 for each item in the list. (Grayed items are optional entries.) If there is a scroll bar to the right of the list, use it to bring additional items into view.

10. Click on the checkmark button. The Formula Composer inserts the function and argument into the selected cell.

   Once you learn the basics of working with functions, you may want to bypass the Formula Composer. You can select a function by clicking on the @ button in the input line. Click on the desired function, and click on OK. You can then type the argument.

Using Logical Operators

In addition to mathematical operators, Quattro Pro allows you to use logical operators. For example, to determine whether a customer has to pay out-of-state sales tax, you can

Lesson 5

use a logical operator along with the IF function in a sales invoice (see Figure 5.3). If the customer's state is specified in cell D17, and the subtotal of the invoice is in cell G29, the statement might read as follows:

@IF(D17=IN,.05*G29,0)

That is, if the state specified in cell D17 is (=) Indiana (**IN**), then (,) multiply the subtotal in cell **G29** by 5% (**.05**); otherwise, enter **0** for the sales tax. Table 5.1 shows a list of logical operators.

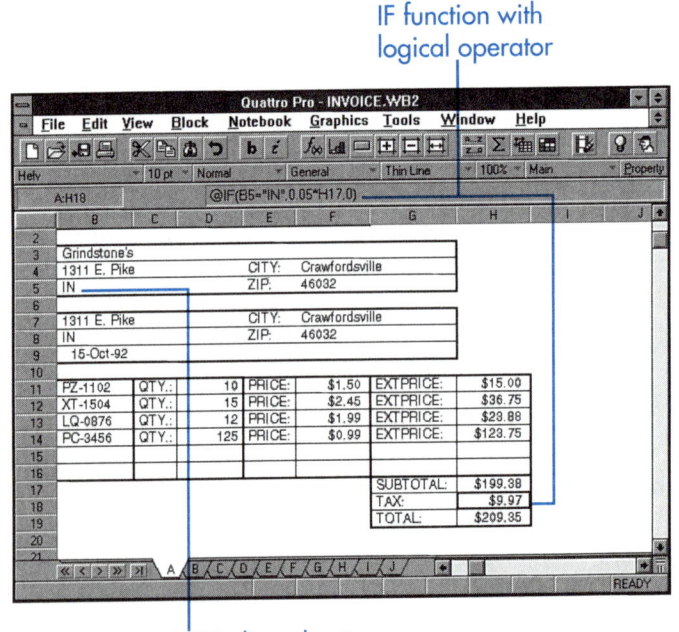

IF function with logical operator

Because B5=IN, the value in H17 is multiplied by .05 to determine tax due.

Figure 5.3 You can use logical operators to define a condition.

Table 5.1 Logical Operators

Operator	Meaning
<	Less than
>	Greater than
<=	Less than or equal to
>=	Greater than or equal to
<>	Less than or greater than but not equal to
=	Equal to
#NOT#	Logical NOT
#AND#	Logical AND
#OR#	Logical OR

In this lesson, you learned how to enter functions to perform complex mathematical and logical equations. In the next lesson, you will learn how to save, close, and open your notebook files.

Lesson 6

Saving, Closing, and Opening Notebooks

In this lesson, you'll learn how to save, close, open, and retrieve spreadsheet notebooks.

Saving Spreadsheet Notebooks

As you work with spreadsheet notebooks, the data you enter is stored only temporarily in your computer's electronic memory—RAM (Random Access Memory). If your computer loses power (or you quit Quattro Pro without saving your work), you lose any data that you have not saved to disk. The following sections explain the different ways to save your notebooks to disk.

Saving a Notebook for the First Time

When you first start Quattro Pro for Windows, the program displays a temporary notebook named NOTEBK1.WB2 with which you can begin working. You can make the notebook file permanent by saving it to disk and giving it a unique name.

The name must consist of a *base name* (up to eight characters), a period, and an *extension* (up to three characters). You cannot use any of the following characters:

space ' + = | \ / <> , { }

Saving, Closing, and Opening Notebooks

If you do not type a period and extension, Quattro Pro will add the extension .WB2 automatically to mark the file as a Quattro Pro file.

Take the following steps to save a notebook file:

1. Pull down the File menu and select Save. The Save File dialog box appears, as shown in Figure 6.1.

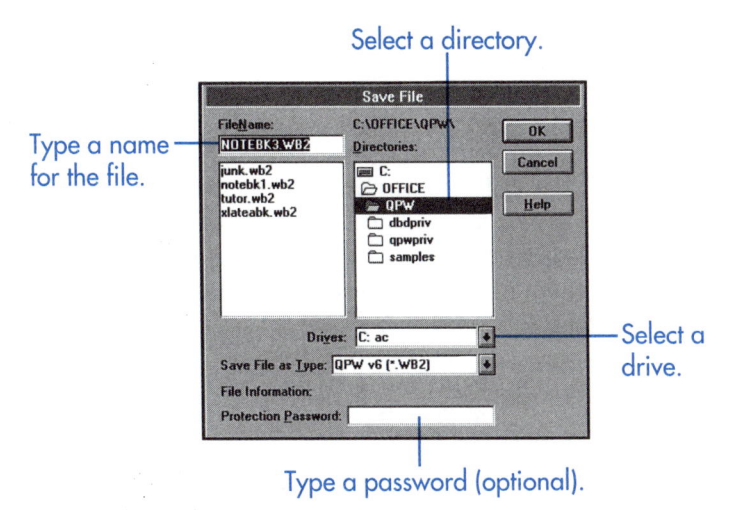

Figure 6.1 The Save File dialog box prompts you to enter a name for the file.

2. To save the notebook under a different name, type the name you want to use. Whatever you type replaces the entry in the FileName text box.

3. To save the file to a different drive, select the drive from the Drives list.

4. To save the file to a different directory, select the directory from the Directories list.

> **Sharing Files** If you plan on using the file you created in a different spreadsheet program, such as Lotus 1-2-3, you can use the Save File as Type list to save the file in a format compatible with the program you intend to use.

5. **(Optional)** To prevent unauthorized people from opening the file, type a password in the Protection Password text box. As you type, pound signs (####) appear so nobody can look over your shoulder and see the password.

6. Click on the OK button to save the file to the specified drive and directory. If you added a password, a dialog box appears, prompting you to confirm. If you added a password, type the same password and press Enter.

As you work with a notebook, you should save the notebook to disk every ten to fifteen minutes to protect your data. Simply click on the Save Notebook button, or open the File menu and select Save. Because you have already named the file, the Save File dialog box does not appear.

Saving a Notebook Under Another Name

Quattro Pro's File menu contains a Save As command which allows you to create a copy of a notebook file. This is useful if you want to create a copy of the notebook and change the copy without affecting the original file. You can also use the Save As command to save the file in a different format, such as Lotus 1-2-3 or Excel without affecting the format of the original file.

Saving, Closing, and Opening Notebooks 33

Closing a Notebook

When you are finished with a notebook, you can close it without exiting the program. To close a notebook, take the following steps:

1. Pull down the File menu and choose Close. If you entered any changes since the last time you saved the notebook, a dialog box appears, asking whether you want to save the changes.

2. Select Yes to save the changes, No to close the notebook without saving the changes, or Cancel to keep the notebook open.

Opening a Notebook

Once you've saved a notebook to disk, you can open the notebook at any time to work with it. To open a notebook file, take the following steps:

1. Pull down the File menu and select Open. The Open File dialog box appears, as shown in Figure 6.2.

Select the name of the file

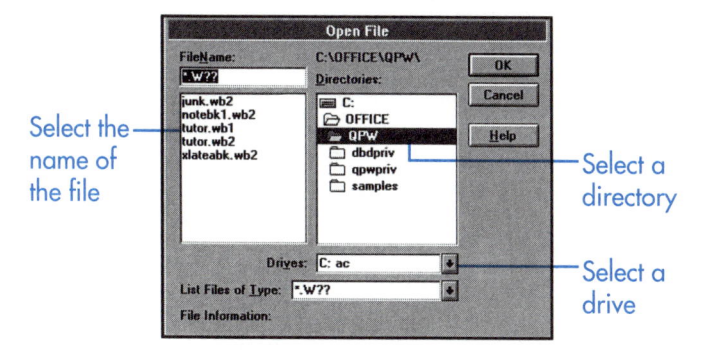

Select a directory

Select a drive

Figure 6.2 The Open File dialog box prompts you to select the file you want to open.

2. Select the drive and directory in which the file is stored.

3. In the FileName list, click on the name of the file you want to open.

> **File Not Listed?** If the file you want to open is not listed, you may have to edit the entry in the FileName text box. Try typing *.* and pressing Enter to view all the files in the selected directory.

4. Click on the OK button. Quattro Pro opens the notebook file in a separate window. (If the file has password protection, type your password and select OK.)

Making a New Notebook

Quattro Pro offers two ways to start a new notebook. You can start with a blank notebook (as you do when you run Quattro Pro), or you can use one of Quattro Pro's templates, including an accounts payable register, auto expenses tracking sheet, product invoice, and more. To create a new notebook, take the following steps:

1. Open the File menu and select New. The New File dialog box appears.

2. Do one of the following:

   Click on Plain Notebook to create a blank notebook.

   Click on From Quick Template, and then click on the desired template in the Quick Templates list.

3. Click on the OK button.

Quick File Options You can set Quattro Pro's default file options by right-clicking in the Quattro Pro title bar and selecting File Options. You can change the default directory Quattro Pro uses to save and open files, turn on the automatic backup feature, and specify a file to load automatically on startup.

Switching Notebook Windows

If you have two or more notebooks open, you can switch from one to the other by selecting the desired window from the Window menu. You can also cycle through the open windows by pressing Ctrl+F6. For more information on working with windows, refer to the Windows primer at the back of this book.

In this lesson, you learned how to save notebook files to disk and how to close and open notebooks. In the next lesson, you will learn how to select cell blocks in order to work with cells as a group.

Lesson 7

Selecting and Naming Cells

In this lesson, you will learn how to select cells in order to work with them as a group, and how to name cells.

Selecting Multiple Cells

In earlier lessons, you selected individual cells in order to type entries into them. Sometimes, however, you will need to work with multiple cells that act as a unit, called a *cell block*. You will usually select a cell block to perform an operation on several cells at the same time. For example, you may want to move or delete several cells, change the character formatting in the cells, or perform a mathematical operation on a group of cells.

> **Cell Block** A cell block is two or more selected cells, as opposed to a single cell. Cell blocks are also referred to as *ranges*.
>
> Plain English

With the mouse, you can select a cell block, a column, a row, or the entire spreadsheet by performing the actions shown in Figure 7.1. To select more than one block, hold down the Ctrl key while selecting blocks. You can select the same block on several consecutive pages of a notebook. Select the block on the first page, hold down the Shift key, and click on the tab for the last page you want included.

Selecting and Naming Cells 37

Click here to select a row.   Click here to select the entire spreadsheet.   Click here to select a column.

Hold down the Ctrl key to select multiple blocks.   Drag over cells to select a block.

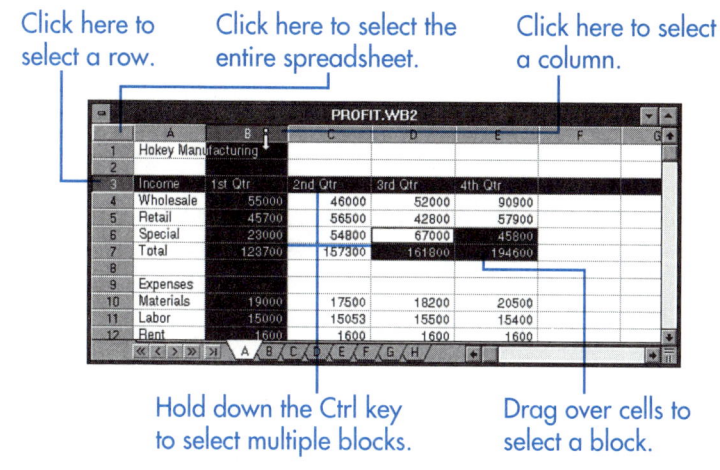

Figure 7.1 The mouse offers intuitive ways to select cell blocks.

Selecting and Moving If you hold down the mouse button too long before you start dragging over cells, the pointer turns into a hand, and you end up moving a cell rather than selecting multiple cells. You can increase the amount of time that it takes for the pointer to turn into a hand. Right-click inside the Quattro Pro title bar, click on General, and enter a larger number in the Cell Drag and Drop Delay Time text box (1000 = 1 second).

With the keyboard, take the following steps to select a block:

1. Move the selector to the first or last cell in the block you want to select.

2. Press Shift+F7. **EXT** appears in the status line, indicating that you are now in Extend mode.

3. Use the arrow keys to stretch the highlight over the cells you want to include in the block. (You can use any of the keys listed in Lesson 2, Table 2.1, to move the selector.)

4. Press F7 to turn off Extend mode.

> **Quick Stretch**   To stretch the highlight quickly over a block of cells, move the selector to the first cell, hold down the Shift key, and use the arrow keys to stretch the highlight.

Specifying Blocks in Dialog Boxes

You will often enter commands in Quattro Pro that prompt you to specify a *range* of cells. For example, if you select Move from the Block menu, a dialog box appears prompting you to specify the range of cells you want to move (see Figure 7.2). The box will contain an entry, such as **A1..A11**, which you can edit. You can either type the range in the text box or select the range by using the arrow keys or the mouse.

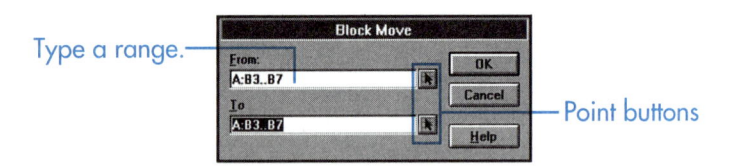

Type a range. ⎯ [Block Move dialog with From: A:B3..B7, To: A:B3..B7, OK, Cancel, Help] ⎯ Point buttons

Figure 7.2   You can type a range to specify a block of cells.

Typing a Range

To specify a range of cells by typing an entry, type the address of the cell in the upper left corner of the block, type two periods, and type the address of the cell in the lower right corner—for example, **D10..D14**. (You can use either one or two periods to separate the cell addresses in an entry.) To specify a range on a different page, precede the range with a page letter and a colon, for example, **C:D10..D14**.

Multiple Blocks To work with more than one block, separate each range with a comma. For example, **A1..A10,C5,D10..E15**.

Using the Point Method

When you encounter a dialog box that prompts you to type a range, you'll see a Point button to the right of the range text box. Instead of typing the range, you can click on this button and then select the range with your mouse. Here's what you do:

1. Click on the Point button to the right of the text box. The dialog box disappears except for the title bar. **POINT** appears on the status line.

2. Drag over the cells you want to include in the block. (To use the keyboard, type a period and use the arrow keys to stretch the highlight.)

3. Press Enter or click on the Maximize button in the dialog box's title bar. The dialog box appears, and the selected range is entered in the text box.

4. If there is another text box that requires you to specify a range, repeat the steps.

Using Named Cells and Ranges

Instead of working with cryptic cell addresses and ranges, you can name individual cells or cell blocks. You can then use the names in formulas and for quickly selecting cell blocks.

Naming Cells

To name a cell or cell block, take the following steps:

1. Select the cell or cell block you want to name.

2. Right-click on the block and select Names. The Block Names dialog box appears, as shown in Figure 7.3.

3. Type a name in the Name text box.

4. Click on the Add button.

5. Click on the Close button.

Type a name here.

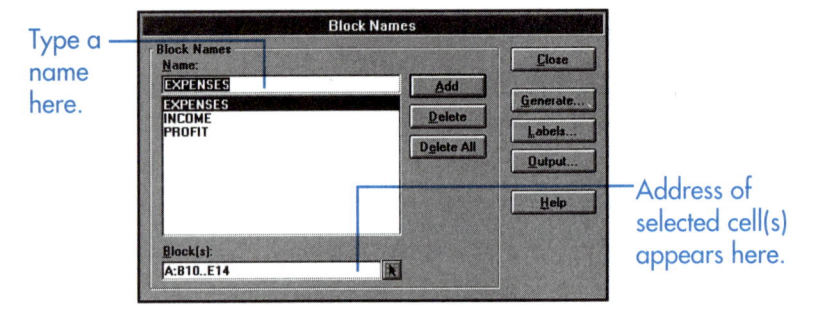

Address of selected cell(s) appears here.

Figure 7.3 The Block Names dialog box lets you name cells and cell blocks.

Using the Point Method You can use the Point method to select the range of cells you want to name. Click inside the Block(s) text box, then click on the Point button. Use your mouse to select the cell(s) you want to name, then click on the Maximize button in the Block Names title bar.

Selecting Cells by Their Names

If you name a block of cells, you can use the name to select a cell block quickly:

1. Press the F5 key or pull down the Edit menu and select Go to. The Go To dialog box appears.

2. Click on the name of the desired cell block in the Block Names list.

3. Click on the OK button. The selector moves to the cell block and selects all the cells in that block.

You can use a cell or range name whenever Quattro Pro prompts you to specify a cell or cell block.

In this lesson, you learned how to select single and multiple cells, and how to name cells. In the next lesson, you will learn how to edit a cell's contents and cut, copy, and paste cells.

Lesson 8

Editing Cells

In this lesson, you'll learn how to edit the contents of cells, how to cut, copy, and paste cells, and how to copy and move cell blocks.

Editing the Contents of a Cell

Once you've entered a label, value, or formula in a cell, you can replace the entry or edit it. To replace the entry, select the cell, type the new entry, and press Enter or click on ✓. To edit the entry, take the following steps:

1. Select the cell whose contents you want to edit. The cell's contents appear on the Input line.

2. Double-click on the cell or click on the entry on the Input line. The insertion point appears.

3. Use the keys listed in Table 8.1 to move the insertion point and edit the entry.

4. Press Enter or click on ✓ to accept the entry, or press Esc or click on X to cancel.

Table 8.1 The Quattro Pro Edit Keys

Press	To
← →	Move the insertion point left or right one character.

Editing Cells

Press	To
Home	Move the insertion point to the beginning of the Input line.
End	Move the insertion point to the end of the Input line.
Del	Delete the character to the right of the insertion point.
Backspace	Delete the character to the left of the insertion point.

Spell-Checking To check your entries for misspellings and typos, open the Tools menu, select Spell Check, and click on the Start button. For more information, click on the Help button when the Spell Check dialog box appears. (You usually spell-check a notebook after typing all your entries.)

Undoing Changes

Whenever you make a change, you have the option of undoing that change, as long as you undo the change immediately. To undo a change, do one of the following:

- Click on the Undo/Redo button in the Toolbar.
- Press Ctrl+Z.
- Open the Edit menu and select Undo.

You can undo the undo operation, as well. Simply open the Edit menu and select Redo, or click on the Undo/Redo button again.

> **Safer Undo** To experiment with a notebook without risk, use the Save As feature to create a copy of the notebook. If you like the changes, use this copy and delete the original. If you don't like the changes, delete the copy and use the original file.

Deleting Cell Contents

If you need to clear data from cells, you can delete the cells' contents or the contents and formatting by performing the following steps:

1. Select the cell(s) whose contents you want to delete.

2. Pull down the Edit menu and select Clear (to delete the contents and remove formatting) or Clear Values (to delete the contents and leave the formatting intact). Refer to Lessons 10 through 12 for details about formatting.

> **Quick Delete** To delete only the contents of cell(s), select the cell and press the Del key. To delete the contents and any formatting, press Shift+Del.

Copying and Moving Cells with Drag and Drop

The quickest way to copy or move selected cells is to drag the selected cell(s) from one location to another using the Drag and Drop feature. This feature does not use the Windows Clipboard, so you can create only a single copy of a block at a time. To use the Drag and Drop feature, perform the following steps:

Editing Cells

1. Select the cell(s) you want to move or copy. (If you are copying a cell block, you must select neighboring cells.)

2. To copy the block, hold down the Ctrl key while performing the following steps.

3. Move the mouse pointer over one of the selected cells and hold down the mouse button until a hand appears, as shown in Figure 8.1.

4. Drag the mouse until the outline of the block is over the block where you want to copy or move the selected cell(s).

> **Don't Move the Block Outline Over Data**
> If you drag the block outline over existing data and release the mouse button, that data is replaced by the copied or moved data. Make sure you copy only to empty cells.

5. Release the mouse button and then the Ctrl key (if you were holding it down). The cell or cell block is copied or moved to the designated location.

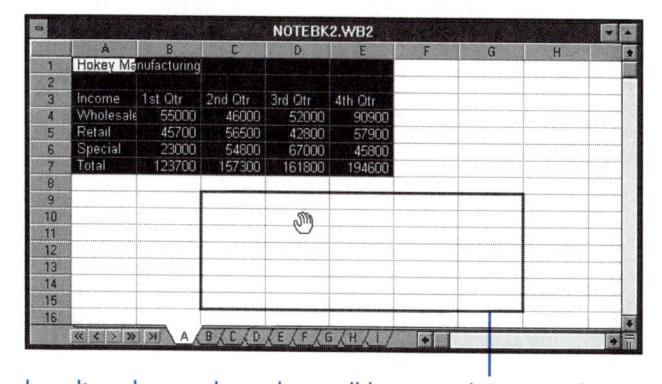

Block outline shows where data will be copied or moved.

Figure 8.1 The Drag and Drop feature lets you copy or move selected cell(s).

Copying and Cutting Cells to the Clipboard

To copy or move cells to another page or to create multiple copies of the same data, use the Copy and Cut commands on the Edit menu. These commands place the contents and formatting of the selected cell(s) on the Windows Clipboard. You can then paste the data from the Clipboard to a new location. To cut or copy cells, perform these steps:

1. Select the cell(s) whose contents you want to cut or copy.

2. Pull down the Edit menu and select Cut or Copy.

> **Quick Cut or Copy** To cut or copy the contents or formatting of the selected cells, click on the Cut or Copy button on the left end of the Toolbar. You can also press Ctrl+X to cut or Ctrl+C to copy.

Pasting Cells from the Clipboard

Once you've put the contents and formatting of a cell or cell block on the Windows Clipboard, you can paste the contents and/or formatting into different cells on the same spreadsheet page, on a different page, or in another notebook. Here's how:

1. Move the selector to the spreadsheet page on which you want to paste the cells' contents.

2. Move the selector to the cell where you want the first cell's contents inserted, or select the cells. The contents will be inserted into the cells starting at the upper left cell and working down and to the right.

Editing Cells 47

3. Pull down the Edit menu and select Paste, or click on the Paste button in the Toolbar.

Paste Special The Paste Special command on the Edit menu allows you to paste either the contents or the formatting (properties) of the copied or cut block. This option also lets you transpose rows and columns so that the data in rows are pasted in columns and the data in columns are pasted in rows.

Copying and Moving Cell Blocks

Another way to copy or move cells is to use the Copy and Move commands on the Block menu. These commands are useful if you are accustomed to working with DOS spreadsheets or if you are moving named blocks. Block commands also work slightly faster than Edit commands; they bypass the Windows Clipboard. Instead of cutting and pasting, you use dialog boxes to specify the cells you want to copy or move to.

In this lesson, you learned how to edit cells and how to copy and move the contents of a cell or cell block from one area of the spreadsheet to another. In the next lesson, you will learn how to control rows and columns.

Lesson 9

Controlling Columns and Rows

In this lesson, you'll learn how to change the column width and row height, and how to insert and delete columns and rows.

Changing the Column Width

If you enter a value—or if a formula calculates a value—that is too wide for the cell it is in, Quattro Pro displays a series of asterisks in place of the value, or displays the numbers in scientific notation (depending on the cell format). If you type a label that is too wide for the cell, Quattro Pro spills the overflow into the next cell (if it's empty), or displays only part of the label. In either case, you'll need to widen the column to display the label or value in its proper format.

Using the Fit Button

The easiest way to set the column width is to use the Fit button. Quattro Pro adjusts the columns to make them one character wider than the widest entry in each column. Take the following steps:

1. Drag over the borders for the columns you want to adjust. (A *column border* is the letter at the top of a column.)

Controlling Columns and Rows   49

2. Click on the Fit button. Quattro Pro adjusts the column widths, displaying complete entries.

> **You Must Readjust** The Fit button adjusts the width of the columns for only the current entries. If you type a wider entry later, you must widen the columns again.

Dragging Column Borders

For greater control over column widths, you can drag the column borders with your mouse:

1. Move the mouse pointer over the right edge of the column border you want to resize. The pointer turns into a double-headed arrow, as shown in Figure 9.1.

2. Hold down the mouse button and drag the mouse to the right to widen the column or to the left to narrow it.

3. Release the mouse button.

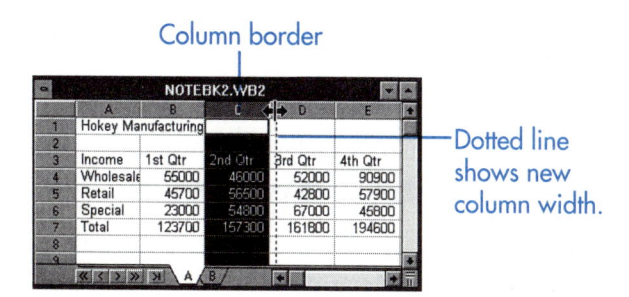

Figure 9.1 Drag the right side of the column border to change its width.

Using the Object Inspector

For more control over column width, right-click on the column border of one of the selected columns, and select Block Properties. This displays the Active Block object inspector. Click on Column Width (see Figure 9.2). Type the number of characters wide you want the column(s) to be, and click on the OK button.

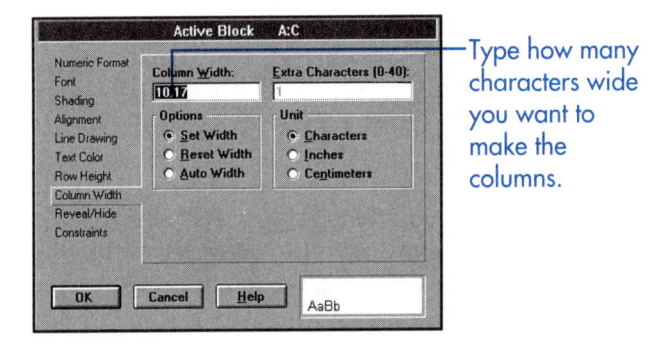

Type how many characters wide you want to make the columns.

Figure 9.2 Use the Column Width settings to widen or narrow a column.

Default Width To change the default column width for a page, right-click on the page tab. Choose Default Width, type your column width setting, and click on OK.

Changing the Row Height

Quattro Pro automatically sets the row height according to the tallest text in the row. You can, however, change the row height. Using the mouse, take the following steps:

1. Move the mouse pointer to the bottom of the row border whose height you want to change. The pointer turns into a double-headed arrow.

Controlling Columns and Rows

2. Hold down the mouse button and drag the mouse down to increase the height or up to decrease the height. (See Figure 9.3.)

3. Release the mouse button.

Row border

Dotted line shows new row height.

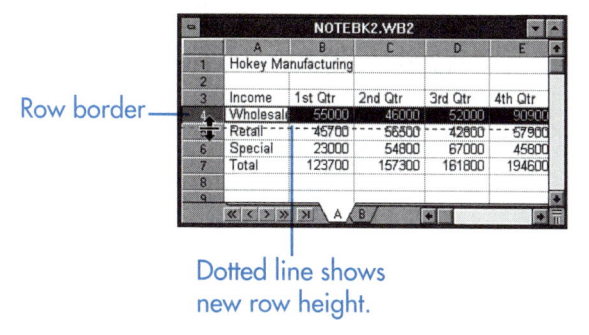

Figure 9.3 Drag the bottom border of the row to change the row's height.

Decreasing Row Height Be careful when decreasing row height. If you make the row shorter than the text, you will chop off the tops of characters.

Although dragging the row with the mouse is the easiest way to change row height, you can make more precise adjustments by using the Active Block object inspector. Simply right-click on the row border whose height you want to change, select Block Properties, click on Row Height, and type a new row height in points (a point is 1/72 of an inch). Click on OK.

Inserting Rows, Columns, or Blocks

As you enter data, you may realize that you need an extra row or column between rows or columns that already contain entries. You can insert one or more rows or columns by performing the following steps:

1. Click on the column border to the right of where you want the new column inserted.

   OR

   Click on the row border below where you want the new row inserted.

   Inserting Multiple Columns or Rows To insert more than one row or column, drag over the number of column or row borders you want to insert.

2. Click on the Insert button. Quattro Pro inserts the row(s) or column(s).

To insert a block of cells rather than an entire row or column, drag over the number of cells you want to insert. (Cells will be inserted above or to the left of the selected cells, and the selected cells will be shifted down or to the right to make room.) Click on the Insert button to display the Block Insert dialog box. Click on Partial in the Span area. In the Dimension area, click on Columns (to shift the selected cells to the right) or Rows (to shift the cells down). Click on OK.

Deleting a Row or Column

You can delete rows and columns as easily as you can insert them. Perform the following steps:

1. Click on the border for the row or column you want to delete, or drag over the borders to delete multiple rows or columns.

2. Click on the Delete button. Quattro Pro removes the selected column(s) or row(s), and shifts surrounding data up or to the left.

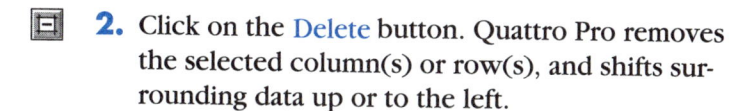

To delete a block of cells instead of a row or column, select the cells, then click on the Delete button. In the Block Delete dialog box that appears, click on Partial in the Span area. In the Dimension area, click on Rows (to shift data from below up into the space left by the deleted cells) or click on Columns (to shift data from the right). Click on OK.

Locking Column and Row Titles

Most spreadsheets are too large for the entire spreadsheet to fit on the screen. When you scroll through the spreadsheet, however, the labels at the top and left sides of the sheet scroll off the screen, preventing you from seeing which rows and columns the displayed values pertain to. To keep the row and column titles on-screen, you can lock them in place:

1. Move the selector to the cell that is to the right of the row titles and/or below the column titles you want to lock. (See Figure 9.4.)

2. Pull down the View menu and select Locked Titles. The Locked Titles dialog box appears.

3. Select Horizontal to lock the column titles, Vertical to lock the row titles, or Both to lock both column and row titles.

4. Click on the OK button.

54   Lesson 9

This column of row titles will be locked.

Cell selector

These rows of column titles will be locked.

	A	B	C	D	E	F	G
1				Merry Melody Sales Figures			
2							
3			Violins	Oboes	Flutes	Pianos	Tubas	Total Sales
4		January	$2,500.00	$1,200.00	$900.00	$1,500.00	$300.00	$6,400.00
5		February	$1,500.00	$1,350.00	$1,200.00	$1,600.00	$600.00	$6,250.00
6		March	$1,300.00	$1,240.00	$1,100.00	$27,000.00	$900.00	$31,540.00
7		April	$1,500.00	$1,250.00	$800.00	$12,000.00	$1,200.00	$16,750.00
8		May	$2,500.00	$1,450.00	$450.00	$13,000.00	$1,500.00	$18,900.00
9		June	$2,200.00	$1,300.00	$230.00	$9,000.00	$1,700.00	$14,430.00
10		July	$1,400.00	$1,250.00	$400.00	$7,000.00	$1,800.00	$11,850.00
11		August	$1,200.00	$1,300.00	$500.00	$5,000.00	$4,500.00	$12,500.00
12		September	$600.00	$1,200.00	$450.00	$15,000.00	$3,400.00	$20,650.00
13		October	$300.00	$1,100.00	$350.00	$21,000.00	$2,300.00	$25,050.00
14		November	$250.00	$1,300.00	$250.00	$13,000.00	$2,400.00	$17,200.00
15		December	$190.00	$1,400.00	$150.00	$12,000.00	$3,400.00	$17,140.00
16							
17							

Figure 9.4 Move the selector below and to the right of the titles you want to lock.

Now, when you scroll through the spreadsheet, the titles will remain in place. To unlock the titles, repeat the steps and select Clear in the Locked Titles dialog box.

In this lesson, you learned how to control the overall layout of your spreadsheet by changing the column width and row height, and by inserting and deleting columns and rows. In the next lesson, you'll learn how to control the appearance of the text within cells.

Lesson 10

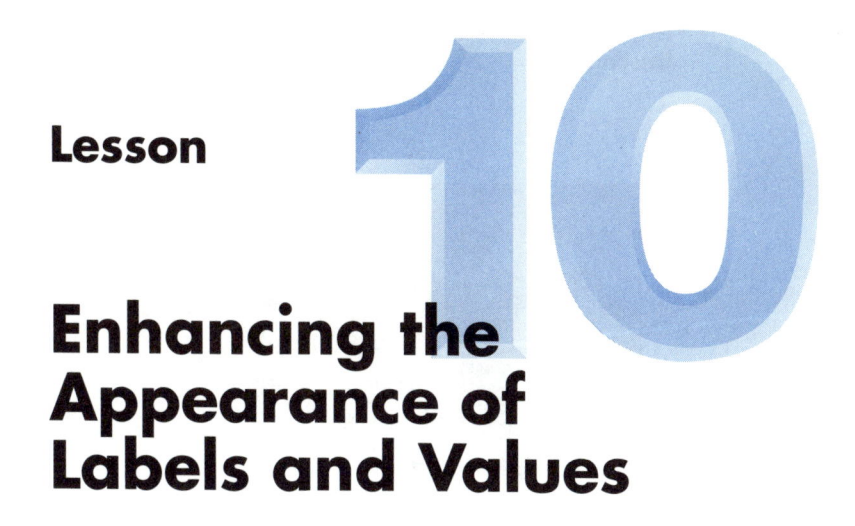

Enhancing the Appearance of Labels and Values

In this lesson, you'll learn how to format values, change fonts, and align text in cells.

Formatting Values

Numeric values are usually more than just numbers. They represent a dollar value, a date, a percent, or some other real value. For example, an entry of 9 can mean 900%, $9.00, or 9:00 a.m. As you learned in Lesson 3, however, spreadsheets don't like you to type the dollar signs and other characters that give values meaning. Instead, you must specify a number *format* by performing the following steps:

1. Select the cell(s) that contain the value(s) you want to format.

2. Right-click on one of the selected cells, and click on Block Properties. The Active Block object inspector appears with Numeric Format selected. A list of numeric formats appears on the right, as shown in Figure 10.1.

3. Select the numeric format you want to use. An example of the selected format is shown in the preview area. A text box or another list of options may appear on the right.

Lesson 10

Select a numeric format.

Other options may appear here.

Selected format in action

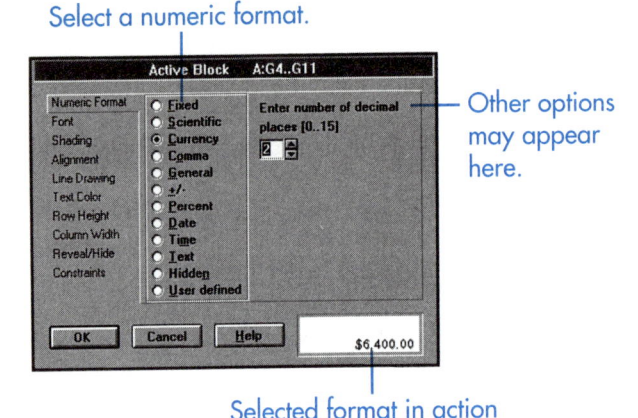

Figure 10.1 Right-click on a selected cell to change its numeric format.

4. If a text box or another list of options appears, select an option or enter the requested information. For example, you can specify the number of decimal places to show, or pick from a list of date formats.

5. Click on the OK button to apply the selected format. You are returned to the notebook, and the value is formatted as specified.

> **Quick Numeric Formats** A quick way to select Comma, Currency, Percent, Fixed, or Date is to pull down the Style list from the Property Band and click on the numeric format you want to use, as shown here:

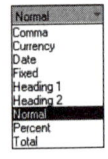

Enhancing the Appearance of Labels and Values   57

Changing Fonts

When you enter a label or value, Quattro Pro uses a default font for the text. You can change the font to improve the overall appearance of the text or to set the text apart from other text.

> **Font** A font is a set of characters that have the same typeface and point size. For example, Helvetica 12-point is a font. Helvetica is the typeface and 12-point is the size. (There are approximately 72 points in an inch.)
>
> *Plain English*

To change fonts, perform the following steps:

1. Select the cell(s) that contain the text whose font you want to change.

2. Right-click on one of the selected cells, and click on Block Properties. The Active Block object inspector appears.

3. Click on Font. A list of available fonts appears, as shown in Figure 10.2.

Select Font. Select a typeface. Select a type size.

Click here to change the text's color.

Select additional attributes.

Preview area

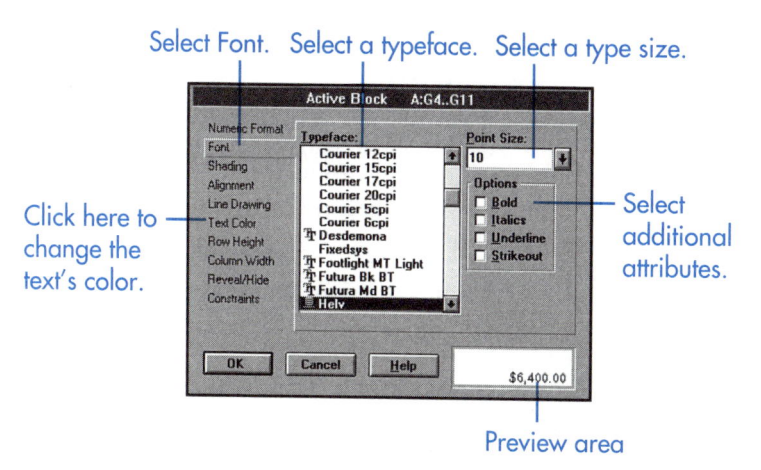

Figure 10.2 You can style your text.

4. Click on the desired typeface in the Typeface list. An example of the selected typeface is shown in the preview area.

5. Use the Point Size drop-down list to select the point size, or type a point size in the text box.

6. To add an attribute to the font, select one or more of the attributes in the Options group: Bold, Italics, Underline, or Strikeout.

7. To change the text's color, click on the Text Color option and select the desired color.

8. Click on the OK button. You are returned to the notebook, and the text is formatted as specified.

> **Quick Styling** You can change fonts and type sizes quickly by selecting from the Font list and Font Size list in the Property Band. To add the bold and/or italic attribute to text, select the cell(s) that contain the text and click on the b or i button in the Toolbar. Clicking on the button once turns the attribute on. Clicking it again turns the attribute off.

Aligning Text in Cells

By default, Quattro Pro uses General alignment to align labels and values in cells: all labels are left-justified and numbers are right-justified. You can change the alignment at any time by performing the following steps:

1. Select the cell(s) whose alignment you want to change.

2. Right-click on one of the selected cells, and click on Block Properties.

Enhancing the Appearance of Labels and Values   59

3. Click on Alignment. A list of alignment options appears, as shown in Figure 10.3.

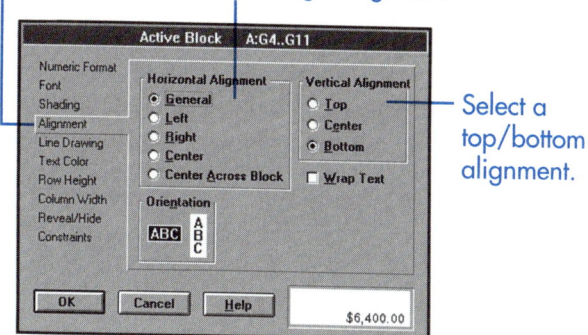

Figure 10.3 Use the Active Block dialog box to align the contents of the selected cell(s).

4. Select the desired alignment option(s). You can select a left/right and top/bottom alignment. You can also turn on Wrap Text to have Quattro Pro place wide entries on multiple lines within a cell.

5. Click on the OK button to apply the selected alignment option. You are returned to the notebook, and the cell contents are aligned as specified.

Quick Alignment A faster way to align text is to select the cells and then choose an alignment from the Align list in the Property Band:

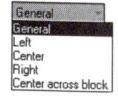

Sometimes it is useful to center a spreadsheet title at the top of a spreadsheet. To do this, select the entire band of cells in which you want the title centered. Pull down the Align list in the Property Band, and click on Center across block.

In this lesson, you learned how to enhance the appearance of a cell's contents by adding a numeric format, by changing fonts and attributes, and by aligning entries in cells. In the next lesson, you will learn how to further enhance your spreadsheet by adding lines and shading.

Lesson 11

Adding Lines and Shading to Cells and Blocks

In this lesson, you'll learn how to enhance your spreadsheet by adding lines and shading to cells or cell blocks.

Drawing Lines Around and Between Cells

As you work with your spreadsheet page on-screen, each cell is identified by a grid line that surrounds the cell. When you print the spreadsheet, however, no lines are printed. To have lines appear on the printout, you must specify where you want the lines to appear and the type of line you want to use. Figure 11.1 shows the options for adding lines to cells and cell blocks.

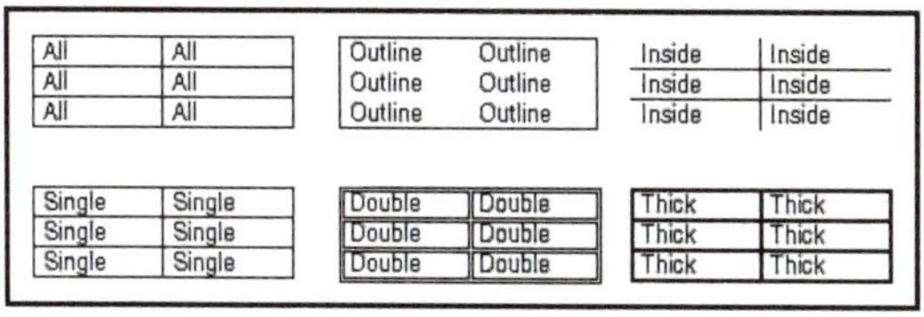

Figure 11.1 Line drawing options.

Lesson 11

To draw lines around or between cells, perform the following steps:

1. Select the cell or cell block where you want the lines to appear.

2. Right-click on one of the selected cells, and select Block Properties. The Active Block object inspector appears.

3. Click on Line Drawing. A list of line drawing options appears on the right, as shown in Figure 11.2.

Pointers show where lines will be added.

Click on a line placement button, or click on the cell boundaries where you want lines added.

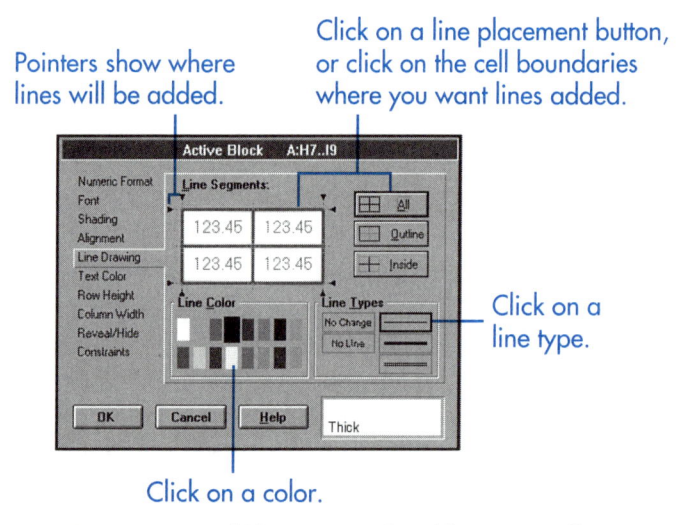

Click on a line type.

Click on a color.

Figure 11.2 You can add lines around and between cells.

4. Click on one of the line placement buttons (All, Outline, or Inside), or click on one or more lines in the Line Segment box to specify where you want the line(s) placed. (If you are using the Line Segments box, hold down the Shift key to select more than one segment.)

5. Click on the desired line type in the Line Types list.

Adding Lines and Shading to Cells and Blocks

6. Click on the desired line color in the Line Color list. If you make no color selection, Quattro Pro uses black.

7. Click on the OK button. You are returned to the notebook, and the selected line type appears around the specified cell(s).

Hiding the Grid Lines

When you start adding your own lines around and between cells, the grid lines that Quattro Pro displays can become distracting. To turn them off, take the following steps:

1. Right-click on the tab for the page whose grid lines you want to hide. The Active Page object inspector appears, showing the Display options.

2. Click on Horizontal and Vertical in the Grid Lines area to turn off the check boxes.

3. Click on the OK button. Quattro Pro hides the grid lines for this page.

To display the grid lines, repeat the steps.

Shading a Cell or Cell Block

Many spreadsheets contain important subtotals and totals that you'll want to highlight in some way. One of the best ways to highlight the contents of any cell is to shade the cell. If you have a color printer, you can shade cells in color. If not, you'll be limited to using gray, black, and white. To add shading to a selected cell or block, perform the following steps:

1. Select the cell or cell block you want to shade.

2. Right-click on one of the selected cells and select Block Properties. The Active Block object inspector appears.

Lesson 11

3. Click on Shading. Two color palettes appear, allowing you to mix colors to create a shade. See Figure 11.3.

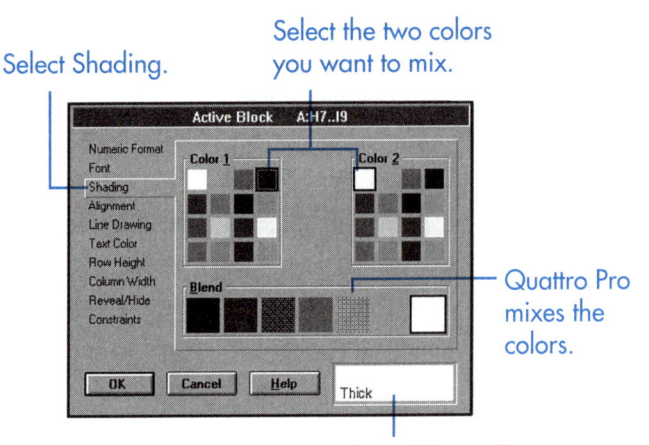

Figure 11.3 You can color or shade your cells.

4. Click on the two colors you want to mix in the Color 1 and Color 2 palettes.

5. Click on the color mix you want to use in the Blend palette. The resulting combination of colors appears in the preview area.

6. Click on the OK button. Quattro Pro applies the shading to the cells.

> **Color Me Invisible** Keep in mind that the shading you select has no effect on the color of the text. By default, the text is black, so if you choose a dark background, you should change the text color, as well. Refer to Lesson 10 for instructions on how to format text.

This lesson explained how to add lines and shading to cells. In the next lesson, you will learn more advanced formatting skills.

Lesson 12

Formatting with SpeedFormat and Styles

In this lesson, you'll learn how to format quickly with SpeedFormat and styles.

Quick Formatting with SpeedFormat

Quattro Pro's SpeedFormat feature allows you to quickly format a table by selecting from several designs. To use SpeedFormat, perform the following steps:

1. Select the block you want to format.

   > **Select Entire Table** You can quickly select all the data on a spreadsheet page. Open the Toolbars list in the Property Band, and select Modeling. Select one cell that contains an entry and then click on the SpeedSelect button in the Modeling toolbar. To redisplay the Main toolbar, open the Toolbars list and select Main.

2. Click on the SpeedFormat button, or right-click on a selected cell and choose SpeedFormat. The SpeedFormat dialog box appears, as shown in Figure 12.1.

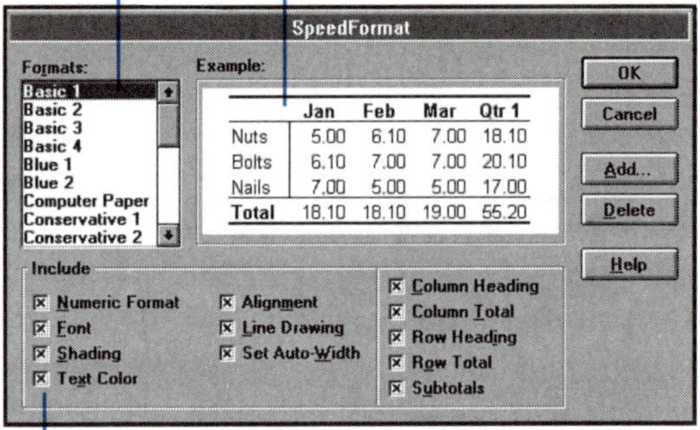

Select a design here. Preview area shows format in action.

Click on a format to turn it off.

Figure 12.1 The SpeedFormat dialog box.

3. Select a design from the Formats list. The preview area displays the selected format.

4. In the Include area, select any formatting option that you want to turn *off*. For example, if you don't want to use lines, click on Line Drawing to remove the X from its check box.

5. Click on the OK button. Quattro Pro closes the SpeedFormat dialog box, and applies the formatting to the selected block.

Understanding Styles

In Lessons 10 and 11, you enhanced a spreadsheet by selecting various formatting options for the cells. Styles allow you to apply several formats to a selected cell or cell block by assigning a named style. Each style contains specifications for text alignment, numeric format, line drawing, shading, font, and text color.

Formatting with SpeedFormat and Styles

Style A style is a group of cell-formatting options you can apply to a cell or cell block. If you change the style's definition later, that change affects the formatting of all cells formatted with that style.

Applying Existing Styles

Quattro Pro comes with several predefined styles, which allow you to add commonly used cell formatting. For example, the HEADING1 style sets the text in Helvetica 18-point bold type. To use one of these styles, or a style you created (explained later), perform the following steps:

1. Select the cell or block you want to format.

2. Pull down the Style list from the Property Band, as shown in Figure 12.2.

3. Select a style from the list. The style is now in effect for the selected cell(s).

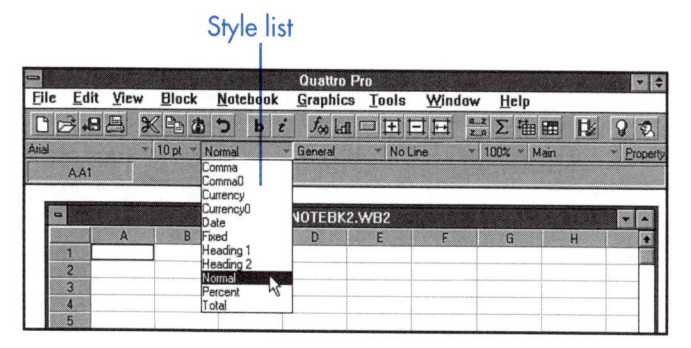

Figure 12.2 Select a style from the Style list.

Removing Formatting A quick way to remove any unwanted formatting from a cell is to select the cell and then select Normal from the Style list.

Creating Custom Styles

In addition to Quattro Pro's existing styles, you can create and use your own styles. To create a style, take the following steps:

1. Open the Notebook menu and select Define Style. The Define/Modify Style dialog box appears as shown in Figure 12.3.

Type a name here.

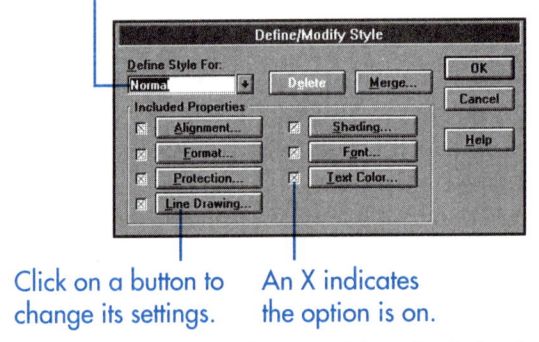

Click on a button to change its settings.

An X indicates the option is on.

Figure 12.3 The Define/Modify Style dialog box.

2. Type a name for the style you want to create in the Define Style For box. The name must differ from any style name currently listed.

3. Click on the button for the format option you want to change. Another dialog box appears, allowing you to change the settings for the selected option.

4. Use the dialog box that appears to change the format settings, and then click on the OK button. This returns you to the Define/Modify Style dialog box. Make sure the option you changed has an X in its check box (meaning the option is on).

5. Repeat steps 3 and 4 for any additional format options you want to change.

Formatting with SpeedFormat and Styles

6. Click on the OK button. Quattro Pro adds the new style to the Style list. You can apply the style by selecting it from the list, as explained in the previous section.

Changing Styles

Styles allow you to change the formatting applied to various cells simply by changing a style's definition. For example, say you use a style called Total to shade a cell and have its text appear in 16-point Times bold. You have used this style on 12 cells (totals and subtotals) throughout the spreadsheet notebook. You later decide that you do not want the cells shaded. All you have to do is change the shading option for the style to no shading; the shading will then be removed from all 12 cells. To change a style, perform the following steps:

1. Open the Notebook menu and select Define Style. The Define/Modify Style dialog box appears (look back at Figure 12.3).

2. Open the Define Style For drop-down list, and select the style you want to change.

3. Click on the button for the formatting option you want to change.

4. Use the dialog box that appears to change the format settings, and then click on the OK button. This returns you to the Define/Modify Style dialog box.

5. Click on the OK button. Quattro Pro applies the new style definition to all the cells you formatted with this style.

In this lesson, you learned how to quickly format a spreadsheet by using SpeedFormat and styles. In the next lesson, you'll learn how to prepare a page for printing.

Lesson 13

Setting Up a Page for Printing

In this lesson, you will learn how to set page margins and add headers and footers for printing your spreadsheet.

Setting Up a Page

Before you print your spreadsheet, you should check Quattro Pro's page settings to make sure the default settings are appropriate for the spreadsheet you want to print. To display the settings, pull down the File menu and select Page Setup. The Spreadsheet Page Setup dialog box appears as in Figure 13.1.

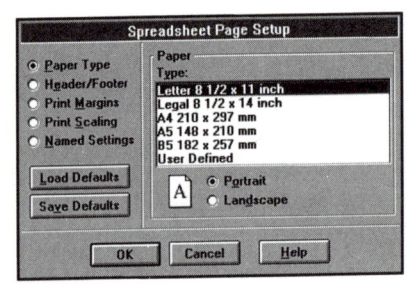

Figure 13.1 Use the Spreadsheet Page Setup dialog box to change the page layout settings.

Setting Up a Page for Printing 71

Printer Setup This lesson assumes you have installed the correct printer driver in Microsoft Windows, and that the currently selected printer is the one you intend to use. To check your printer setup, open the Main group window in the Program Manager, double-click on the Control Panel icon, and double-click on the Printers icon.

Selecting a Paper Type and Orientation

If you use two or more types of paper in your printer, or you want to print sideways on a page (for a printout that is wider than it is tall), you should check the paper type and orientation settings. To check the paper type or orientation, take the following steps:

1. Pull down the File menu and select Page Setup. The Spreadsheet Page Setup dialog box appears (see Figure 13.1).

2. Make sure the correct paper size is selected in the Paper Type list. (You can create a custom size by selecting User Defined.)

3. Select Portrait or Landscape to specify an orientation. Portrait prints the text as in a business letter. Landscape rotates the text 90 degrees, so it prints sideways on a page.

4. Click on the OK button or press Enter to confirm the changes and close the Spreadsheet Page Setup dialog box. You can also leave the dialog box on-screen so you can quickly change other settings discussed in this lesson.

Lesson 13

> **Printer Woes?** If no paper types are listed or if you cannot select an orientation option, those options may not be available for the printer you have. If you know that your printer supports the options, check your printer setup. Pull down the File menu, select Print, and click on the Select Printer button. The dialog box that appears lets you select a printer and change options for that printer.

Adding a Header and Footer

A *header* is any text that appears at the top of every page. It can include the notebook name, the date, page numbers, or any other text. A *footer* is any text that appears at the bottom of every page. To add a header or footer, take the following steps:

1. Pull down the File menu and select Page Setup. The Spreadsheet Page Setup dialog box appears.

2. Select Header/Footer. The Header and Footer text boxes appear on the right (see Figure 13.2).

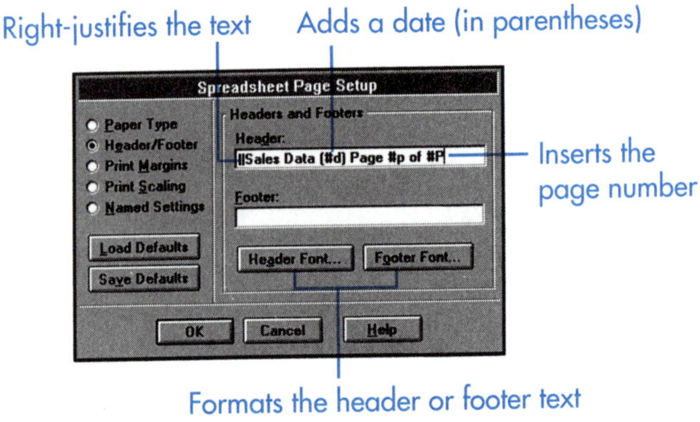

Right-justifies the text — Adds a date (in parentheses)

Inserts the page number

Formats the header or footer text

Figure 13.2 Type a header and/or footer to have it print on your spreadsheet.

Setting Up a Page for Printing

3. Click inside the Header or Footer text box. You can add a header, a footer, or both.

4. Type the text that you want to appear in the header or footer. You can add any of the following codes:

   #p Inserts the correct page number on each page.

   #P Inserts the total number of pages.

   #d Inserts the current date.

   | Centers the text.

   || Right-justifies the text.

5. To change the font for the header or footer, choose the Header Font or Footer Font button. From the dialog box that appears, select a font, type size, and optional attributes, and click on the OK button to return to the Spreadsheet Page Setup dialog box.

6. Click on the OK button.

Setting the Margins

By default, Quattro Pro uses .40-inch left and right margins and .33-inch top and bottom margins. The header is printed .5 inch from the top of the page, and the footer is printed .5 inch from the bottom of the page. To change the margins, take the following steps:

1. Pull down the File menu and select Page Setup. The Spreadsheet Page Setup dialog box appears.

2. Select Print Margins. The margin settings appear on the right.

3. Select Top, Left, Right, or Bottom, and type the margin setting you want to use in inches. (Repeat this step to change additional settings.)

4. To change the placement of the header or footer, select Header or Footer, and type the distance you want the header or footer printed from the top or bottom edge of the page.

5. **(Optional)** If you are printing a long spreadsheet on continuous form paper, you can click on Break Pages to remove the X from the check box.

6. Click on the OK button to confirm your changes and close the dialog box.

> **Breaking Pages** If Quattro Pro breaks pages at an awkward point, you can add your own page breaks. Move the selector to the row just below where you want the page to break. Pull down the Edit menu and select Insert Break. A row is inserted above the selector and four dots appear indicating a page break. To remove the page break, delete the row that contains the page break marker.

Scaling Your Spreadsheet

Quattro Pro can scale your spreadsheet to fit on as few pages as possible, or it can shrink or enlarge the spreadsheet from 1 to 1000 percent its current size. Here's what you do:

1. Pull down the File menu and select Page Setup.

2. Select Print Scaling. The scaling settings appear on the right.

Setting Up a Page for Printing

3. Click on Print to Fit (to print the spreadsheet on as few pages as possible),

OR

Double-click inside the Scaling text box and type a scaling percent from 1 to 1000. (A setting of 70 would shrink the spreadsheet by 30%. A setting of 200 would double the spreadsheet size.)

4. Double click on the OK button.

> **Saving Your Page Setup Settings** You can save your page setup settings to use in other notebooks. After entering your settings, click on the Named Settings option, type a name for the settings, and click on Add. To use the settings, display the Page Setup dialog box, click on Named Settings, select the named setting, and click on Use.

In this lesson, you learned how to set up a page for printing. In the next lesson, you will learn how to print your notebook or a selected portion of the notebook.

Lesson 14

Printing Your Spreadsheet

In this lesson, you will learn how to print an entire notebook, a page, or a selected block.

Quick Printing

If you want to print a selected block or an entire page without any fancy printing options, perform the following steps (you can learn about the fancy printing options later):

1. Make sure your printer is on, has paper, and that the Online light is lit.

2. Click on the tab for the notebook page you want to print.

3. If you do not want to print all the data on the page, select the cells you want to print.

4. Open the File menu and select Print. The Spreadsheet Print dialog box appears, as shown in Figure 14.1.

5. Click on the OK button. Quattro Pro prints the current page or selection.

> **Speedy Printing** To bypass the Spreadsheet Print dialog box, click on the Print button in the Toolbar.

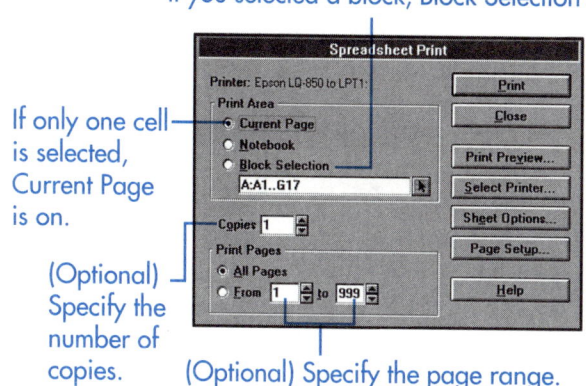

Printing Your Spreadsheet   77

If you selected a block, Block Selection is on.

If only one cell is selected, Current Page is on.

(Optional) Specify the number of copies.

(Optional) Specify the page range.

Figure 14.1 The Spreadsheet Print dialog box.

Previewing Your Printout

Before you print your spreadsheet, it's a good idea to preview it to determine whether it will print correctly. To preview the printout, take the following steps:

1. Open the *File* menu and select *Print Preview*. The first page of your spreadsheet appears in the Preview window, as shown in Figure 14.2.

2. To view the next or previous page of the printout, click on either the *Previous Page* or *Next Page* button.

> **Chopped Text** Don't panic if parts of your words and values are chopped off. In the full page view, Quattro Pro cannot display everything. When you zoom in on the page, as explained next, the text will appear complete.

Lesson 14

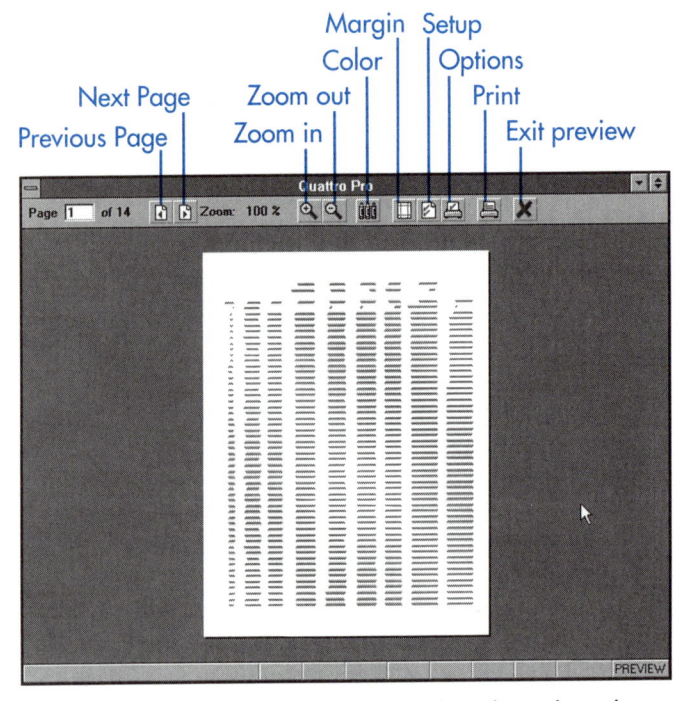

Figure 14.2 The Print Preview window shows how the spreadsheet will appear in print.

(Labels on figure: Previous Page, Next Page, Zoom in, Zoom out, Margin Color, Setup Options, Print, Exit preview)

3. To enlarge the page display, click on the Zoom in button. To shrink the display, click on the Zoom out button. (You can quickly zoom in by left-clicking on an area, or zoom out by right-clicking.)

4. Click on the Color button to toggle the color display on or off. For example, if you used color text, you can see how the color will appear on a black-and-white printer.

5. To adjust the margins, click on the Margin button; when dotted lines appear, drag them to the desired locations.

6. To leave Print Preview, press Esc or click on the Exit preview button.

Printing Your Spreadsheet 79

Setup, Options, and Print Buttons The Setup button displays the Page Setup dialog box explained in Lesson 13. Options displays the Spreadsheet Print Options dialog box explained later in this lesson. The Print button starts printing from the Preview window.

Selecting Special Print Options

Quattro Pro offers several options that give you even more control over your printing. For example, you can have a specific row or column of entries printed on every page, print gridlines, or center the printout on a page. To print a spreadsheet with these special settings, take the following steps:

1. To print only a portion of data, select the desired cells.

2. Open the File menu and select Print. The Spreadsheet Print dialog box appears (look back at Figure 14.1.)

3. Click on the Sheet Options button. The Spreadsheet Print Options dialog box appears, as shown in Figure 14.3.

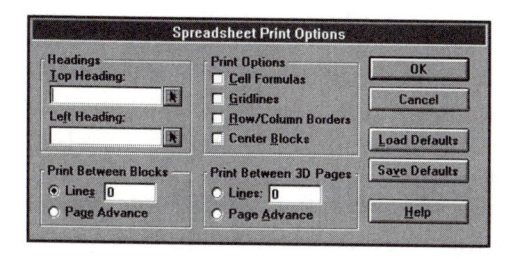

Figure 14.3 Use the Spreadsheet Print Options dialog box to control the print process.

4. Select one or both of the following options to repeat column or row headings on every page:

> **Top Heading:** To have one or more rows repeat, click on the Point button to the right of the Top Heading box, drag over the desired row borders, and click on the Maximize button.
>
> **Left Heading:** To have one or more columns repeat, click on the Point button to the right of the Left Heading box, drag over the desired column borders, and click on the Maximize button.

5. Select any of the following Print Options:

> **Cell Formulas:** Quattro Pro prints the formulas, rather than the results of the formulas.
>
> **Gridlines:** Turn this on to print the gridlines that normally appear only on the display.
>
> **Row/Column Borders:** Turn this on if you want column letters and row numbers printed.
>
> **Center Blocks:** Turn this on to have the printout centered on the page.

6. If you selected more than one cell block to print, choose one of the following Print Between Blocks options:

> **Lines:** Inserts the specified number of line spaces between the blocks. Type the desired number in the Lines text box.
>
> **Page Advance:** Starts each block on a separate page.

Printing Your Spreadsheet

7. If you selected a block on more than one notebook page, choose one of the following Print Between 3D Pages options:

> **Lines:** Inserts the specified number of line spaces between the blocks. Type the desired number in the Lines text box.
>
> **Page Advance:** Starts each block on a separate page.

Save Defaults and Load Defaults If you plan on using the same Sheet Options to print other notebooks, click on the Save Defaults button. You can then use the Load Defaults button whenever you want to use the default settings you saved.

8. Click on the OK button. Quattro Pro returns you to the Spreadsheet Print dialog box.

9. Click on the Print button to start printing.

In this lesson, you learned how to print a spreadsheet quickly, preview a spreadsheet before printing, and enter special print settings. In the next lesson, you will learn how to work with notebook pages.

Lesson 15

Working with Notebook Pages

In this lesson, you'll learn how to select, name, and group notebook pages, and enter notebook page settings.

Working with Notebook Pages

In earlier lessons, you worked with individual cells or cell blocks on a single notebook page. However, you may want to work on more than one page in a notebook. You may want to name the pages, apply formatting to several pages at once, or type the same entry on several pages. In this lesson, you'll learn the basics of working with notebook pages.

Naming Notebook Pages

When you open a notebook for the first time, the tabs at the bottom of the notebook window contain letters. You can replace the letters with names. Whenever you refer to a page, you can then use the name rather than the letter to tell Quattro Pro which page to use. To name the pages, take the following steps:

1. Right-click on the tab you want to name. The Active Page object inspector appears.

2. Click on the Name option. The Page Name text box appears, as shown in Figure 15.1.

Working with Notebook Pages 83

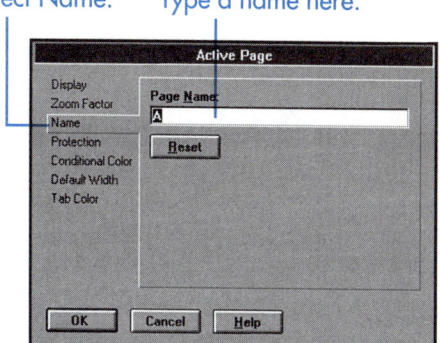

Select Name.   Type a name here.

Figure 15.1   The Active Page object inspector lets you name a page.

3. Type a name for the page (up to 63 characters, no spaces) in the Page Name text box. When you start typing, whatever you type replaces the letter in the text box.

4. Click on the OK button. You are returned to the notebook. The name you typed replaces the letter on the tab.

Changing Notebook Page Settings

The Active Page object inspector, shown in Figure 15.1, contains several other options for controlling notebook pages. Following is a rundown of those options:

Display allows you to turn off the display of column and row borders (to increase screen space) and turn off grid lines. By choosing No in the Display Zeros area, you can hide any zero values in a spreadsheet.

Zoom Factor controls the display size of a notebook. You can zoom in to display text larger or zoom out to see more entries. A quicker way to zoom in and out is to select a percent from the Zoom Factor list in the Property Band.

Protection locks cells or objects on an entire page so nobody can edit the data. To lock or unlock individual cells, right-click on the cells, select Block Properties, select Constraints, and click on Protect or Unprotect.

Conditional Color tells Quattro Pro to display values that fall within a certain range in a specific color. For example, you may want Quattro Pro to display a negative profit number in red.

Default Width allows you to set the default column width for the page in characters, inches, or centimeters. You can still set the column width for individual columns as you create the spreadsheet; this option just tells Quattro Pro the starting width to use.

Tab Color controls the color used for the page tab.

Working with Groups of Pages

Although you will usually work with individual pages, you can often save time by working with several pages at once. For example, you can hide the grid lines on several pages with a single command. To select a group of pages, take the following steps:

1. Click on the tab for the first page you want included in the group.

2. Hold down the Shift key while clicking on the last tab you want in the group. A black line appears under the tabs to show which pages are included in the group.

Working with Notebook Pages 85

> **Keyboard Grouping** To select multiple pages with the keyboard, hold down both the Ctrl key and the Shift key while pressing PgUp or PgDn.

Any formatting change you enter on the current page now affects all pages in the group. You can even enter the same information on several pages, as explained later in this lesson.

You can permanently group pages by naming the group. Here's what you do:

1. Select the pages you want to group, as explained previously.

2. Open the Notebook menu and select Define Group. The Define/Modify Group dialog box appears, as in Figure 15.2.

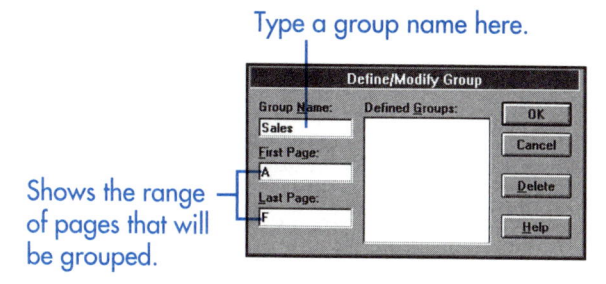

Type a group name here.

Shows the range of pages that will be grouped.

Figure 15.2 You can group and ungroup pages.

3. Type a name for the group and click on the OK button.

4. To activate the group, open the View menu and select Group Mode, or press Alt+F5. A blue line appears below the group.

In Group mode, any formatting you apply to one page in the group is applied to all pages in the group. To ungroup the pages, open the View menu and select Group Mode, or press Alt+F5.

> **Selective Groups** Although you can create more than one group of pages, the changes you make on a page affect only the pages in the current group. For example, if you have two groups of pages, A–C and F–L, and you enter a change on page A, the change will affect only pages A–C, not pages F–L.

Drilling Entries on Groups of Pages

In Group mode, you can enter the same data on all the pages in the group by entering the data on only the first page. Quattro Pro refers to this process as *drilling* an entry. To drill an entry, take the following steps:

1. Turn on Group mode as explained in the previous section.

2. Flip to the first page in the group.

3. Type your entry in the desired cell.

4. Press Ctrl+Enter. The entry is inserted from the input line into the current cell on all pages in the group.

In this lesson, you learned how to name and group notebook pages, as well as how to control their appearance and default settings. In the next lesson, you will learn how to create a graph.

Lesson 16

Creating Graphs

In this lesson, you will learn how to graph your spreadsheet data, resize and move a graph, and change the graph type.

Understanding Quattro Pro's Graph Types and Terminology

With Quattro Pro, you can create various types of graphs, as shown in Figure 16.1. The graph type you choose depends on your data and on how you want to present that data. These are the major graph types and their purposes:

- **Pie** shows the relationship between parts of a whole.
- **Bar** compares values at a given point in time.
- **Line** emphasizes trends and the change of values over time.
- **Area** reveals differences in volumes or amounts.
- **High-Low** shows the high price, low price, and closing price, usually for a stock or commodity.

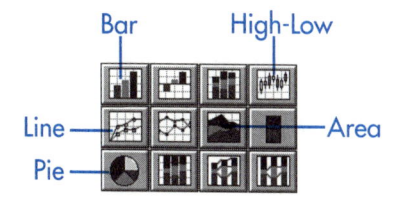

Figure 16.1 Quattro Pro graph types.

The following terminology applies to all types of graphs:

Data Series   A collection of related data, such as the monthly sales for a single division. A data series is usually a single row or column on the spreadsheet.

Axis   One side of a graph. In a two-dimensional graph, there is an *x-axis* (horizontal) and a *y-axis* (vertical). In a three-dimensional graph, the *z-axis* represents the vertical plane, and the x-axis (distance) and y-axis (width) represent the two sides on the floor of the graph.

Legend   Defines the separate elements of a graph. For example, the legend for a pie graph will show what each piece of the pie represents.

Using the Graph Expert

The easiest way to create a graph is to use Quattro Pro's Graph Expert. This tool displays five dialog boxes that lead you through the process of graphing your data. In each dialog box, you enter your preferences and then click on the Next button.

Delete Blank Columns or Rows   Before graphing your data, delete any blank columns or rows in the block you want to graph. Otherwise, these blank rows may enter zero values that will cause problems.

Take the following steps to graph your data:

1. Select the data you want to graph. To place column or row labels on the axes, include them in your selection.

Creating Graphs   89

2. Click on the Experts button. The Experts dialog box appears.

3. Click on the Graph Expert button. The Graph Expert - Step 1 of 5 dialog box appears, as shown in Figure 16.2. The preview area shows how the selected data will be graphed.

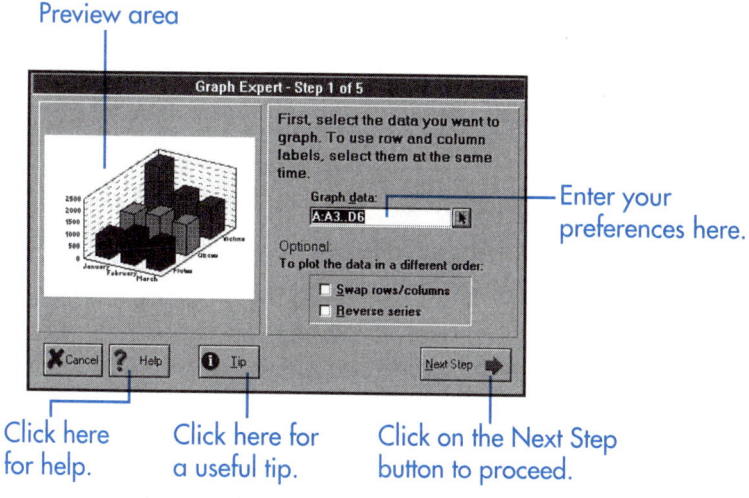

Figure 16.2 The Graph Expert leads you through the process.

4. Perform either or neither of the following actions:

   To graph different data, click on the Point button, drag over the desired data, and click on the Maximize button.

   Click on Swap rows/columns or Reverse series and experiment with different combinations of these options until the graph displays the data as desired.

5. Click on the Next Step button. The Step 2 of 5 dialog box appears, prompting you to select a graph type.

6. Click on the button for the desired graph type, and click on the Next Step button. The Step 3 of 5 dialog box appears, prompting you to select a more specific graph type.

7. Click on a specific graph type, and then click on the Next Step button. The Step 4 of 5 dialog box appears, prompting you to select a color scheme.

8. Click on the desired color scheme, and then click on the Next Step button. The Step 5 of 5 dialog box appears, allowing you to enter titles and prompting you to select a destination for the graph.

9. **(Optional)** To add a title or subtitle, or to name the X- or Y-axis, click inside the appropriate text box and type a label.

10. Select Notebook Page or Graph Window to specify where you want the graph placed. Notebook Page creates a floating graph on the current page. Graph Window places the graph in a separate window where you can customize the graph.

11. Click on the Create Graph button. Quattro Pro graphs your data and inserts the graph where specified.

> **Quick Graphing** To create a quick graph, drag over the data you want to graph, click on the Graph tool button and then click where you want the upper left corner of the graph placed. You can then double-click on the graph to edit it.

Moving and Resizing a Graph

When you select a graph frame, eight *handles* appear around the frame (see Figure 16.3). You can use these handles to change the size and dimensions of the graph frame in the following ways:

- Drag a corner handle to change the width and height of the frame.

- Drag a side handle to change only the width of the frame.

- Drag a top or bottom handle to change only the height of the frame.

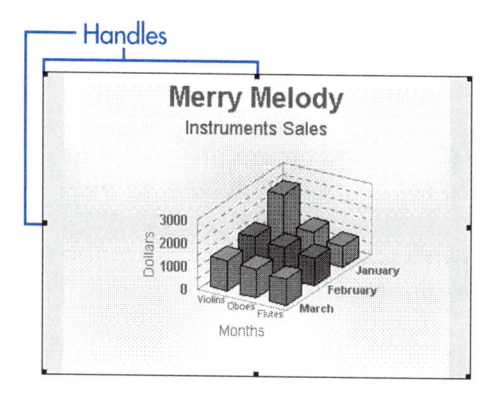

Figure 16.3 Handles allow you to resize and reshape the graph.

To move a graph frame, position the mouse pointer anywhere inside the frame (not on a handle), hold down the mouse button until the hand pointer appears, and drag the frame where you want it. As you drag the frame, a dotted line shows the new location of the frame.

Modifying a Graph

Although the Graph Expert allows you to enter all your preferences for creating a graph, you might need to modify the graph later. For example, you may want to use a different graph type or add a title. To modify the graph, click on it, pull down the Graphics menu, and select one of the following options:

Type allows you to select a different graph type. Click on a general category in the left column, and then choose a specific type on the right.

Series displays a dialog box that allows you to select different data to graph. You can type ranges or use the Point buttons.

Titles lets you enter or edit graph titles and axis labels.

Edit Graph displays the graph in a separate window and provides a Toolbar you can use for editing the graph. See Lesson 17 for details.

View Graph displays the graph in full-screen view. Press Esc to return to the notebook display.

Delete Graph removes the graph from the notebook so you can start over.

Graph Gallery provides another way to change the graph type. This dialog box also allows you to change the color scheme used for the graph. (See Figure 16.4.)

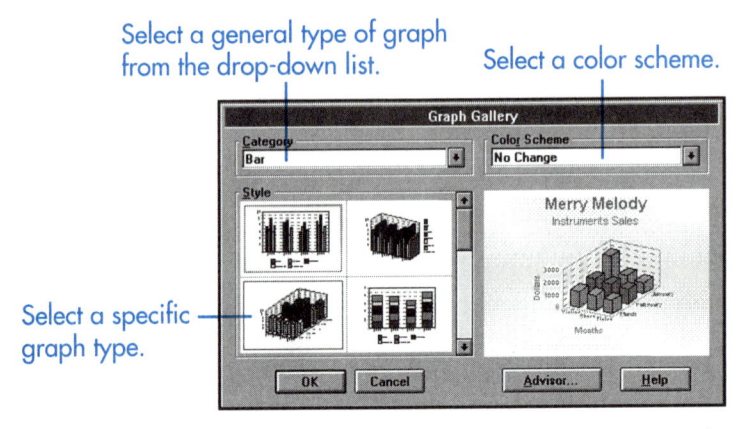

Figure 16.4 The Graph Gallery lets you select a graph type and color scheme.

Lesson 17

Enhancing and Printing Graphs

In this lesson, you will learn how to fine-tune the appearance of a graph, add lines and other graphic objects, and print your graphs.

Displaying a Graph in the Edit Window

At the end of Lesson 16, you learned how to change a graph's overall look by selecting options from the Graphics menu. In this lesson, you will learn how to modify specific parts of a graph, such as a title or axis. In order to make these fine adjustments, however, you must first display the graph in its edit window. Perform one of the following steps:

- Double-click on the graph you want to edit. A blue-hatched border appears around the graph, and the Graph Toolbar appears.

- Open the Graphics menu, select Edit Graph, select the name of the graph you want to edit, and click on the OK button.

- Double-click on the graph icon for the graph you want to edit. (The graph icons are on the last page in the notebook. To move to this page, click on the SpeedTab button.)

If you performed either of the last two steps, the graph appears in an edit window, and the Graph Toolbar appears, as shown in Figure 17.1. To enlarge the view of the graph, click on the Maximize button in the upper right corner of the graph's window.

Figure 17.1 The Graph Edit window allows you to customize your graph.

Customizing a Graph with Object Inspectors

Every graph is made up of *objects*: titles, labels, bars, axes, and so on. Click on various objects now to display the handles that define the objects. The left end of the Input line displays the name of the selected object. Each object has a corresponding *object inspector* that allows you to change its properties, including the object's color, font, and overall appearance. To change the properties of an object, perform the following steps:

Enhancing and Printing Graphs   95

1. Display the graph in its own edit window, as explained in the previous section.

2. Right-click on the object whose look you want to change. Handles appear around the object, and Quattro Pro displays a pop-up menu with the commands you can enter for that object.

3. Click on the Properties option at the top of the pop-up menu. (The Properties option name differs depending on the object.) An object inspector appears. Figure 17.2 shows the object inspector that appears if you right-click on the background area and choose Graph Setup and Background Properties.

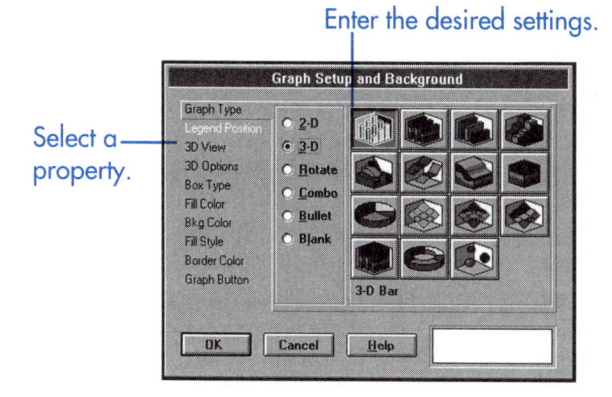

Select a property.

Enter the desired settings.

Figure 17.2 Each object in a graph has its own properties.

4. Click on the property you want to change. The settings for the selected property appear on the right.

5. Select a setting for the property, or enter the required information.

Lesson 17

6. Repeat steps 3 and 4 for all the properties you want to change.

7. Click on the OK button.

> **Using the Property List** Instead of right-clicking on an object, you can open the Property list (in the Property Band) and click on the property you want to change.

Adding Graphic Objects

When you display a graph in its edit window, Quattro Pro displays the Graph Toolbar, which has several tools for drawing lines, arrows, text boxes, circles, and other graphic objects. The procedure for using most of these tools is the same:

1. Click on the button for the tool you want to use. You can select any of the line or shape buttons or the Text tool button.

2. Move the mouse pointer where you want the upper left corner of the object to appear.

3. Hold down the mouse button and drag the mouse until the object is the desired size and dimensions, as shown in Figure 17.3.

Put the mouse pointer here, and hold down the mouse button.

Drag the mouse pointer down and to the right.

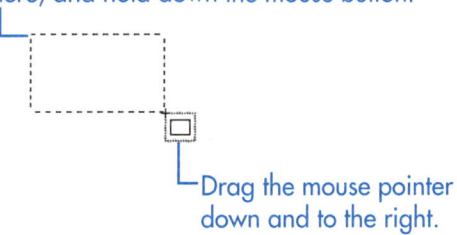

Figure 17.3 Select a drawing tool, then drag the object into existence.

4. Release the mouse button. The object is placed on the page. If you created a text box, proceed to step 5 to enter text.

   Polyline and Polygon Tools Unlike other tools that require a single dragging action, the Polyline and Polygon tools create shapes that consist of several line segments. You must drag each line segment, and then click to end it. Click back at the starting point to close the shape and finish the drawing.

5. Start typing the text you want to appear in the text box.

6. Click anywhere outside the text box when you are done.

Just as you can change the properties for graph objects, you can change properties for any of the objects you add. Right-click on the object and select the Properties option at the top of the menu.

Selecting Objects

Each object you draw is a separate object, which you can delete or modify. To select an object, take the following steps:

1. Click on the Selection tool button.

2. Click on the object you want to select. Handles appear around the selected object.

Selecting Multiple Objects To select several objects, use the mouse pointer to drag a box around the objects you want to select, or hold down the Shift key while clicking on each object. This is useful if you need to move several objects and retain their relative positions. To keep the objects grouped, pull down the Tools menu and select Group.

Once you have selected an object, you can perform several operations on the object:

- To delete an object, press the Del key.
- To move an object, drag it with the mouse.
- To size an object, move the mouse pointer over one of the object's handles, hold down the mouse button, and drag the handle.

Working with Layers of Graphics

As you add graphic objects, some objects may end up hiding other objects. If you need to work with a particular object, you may have to send other objects to the back, or bring the objects you want to work with to the front. To rearrange objects in this way, select the object(s), open the Tools menu, select Object Order, and choose one of the following commands:

Bring Forward moves the selected objects one layer up, but not necessarily to the top.

Send Backward moves the selected objects one layer down, but not necessarily to the very back.

Bring to Front moves the selected objects to the top.

Send to Back moves selected objects to the back.

Align and Palette Toolbars The Align Toolbar has several buttons that allow you to relayer objects without using the Tools menu. To turn on this Toolbar, open the Toolbar list (in the Property Band), and select Align. You can also turn on the Palette Toolbar to change an object's color quickly.

Printing a Graph

You can print a graph in either of two ways: as part of a spreadsheet or by itself. To print the graph as part of the spreadsheet, place the graph on the spreadsheet and then print the spreadsheet, as explained in Lesson 14. To print the graph on a page of its own, you can print from the graph's edit window. Perform the following steps:

1. Double-click on the graph. The graph must be displayed in an edit window or have a blue hatch border around it.

2. Open the File menu and select Print. The Graph Print dialog box appears.

3. Click on the Print button.

In this lesson, you learned how to change the properties of the various objects that make up a graph, add graphic objects, and print your graph. In the next lesson, you will learn how to assemble graphs into a slide show.

Lesson 18

Creating a Slide Show

In this lesson, you will learn how to create a bullet chart and how to assemble graphs and charts to create a slide show.

What Is a Slide Show?

A *slide show* is a frame-by-frame presentation commonly used by marketing and sales departments to help their audiences understand complex data. In the past, you needed a special business-presentation application, such as PowerPoint or Harvard Graphics, to create slide shows. Now, you can create slide shows in many high-end spreadsheet applications, including Quattro Pro.

Creating a Bullet Chart

Although you can create a slide show using only the graphs you created in Lesson 16, you may want to include bullet charts, as well. To create a bullet chart, perform the following steps:

1. On a separate notebook page or on a blank area of the current page, type the following entries (see Figure 18.1):

> **Chart title:** Type the title at the top of the leftmost column.
>
> **Optional subtitle:** Type the subtitle directly below the title in the same column.

Creating a Slide Show   101

Bulleted items: Type a list of major bulleted items one column over and one row down from the subtitle. To include minor bulleted items, type them one row to the right of the major items.

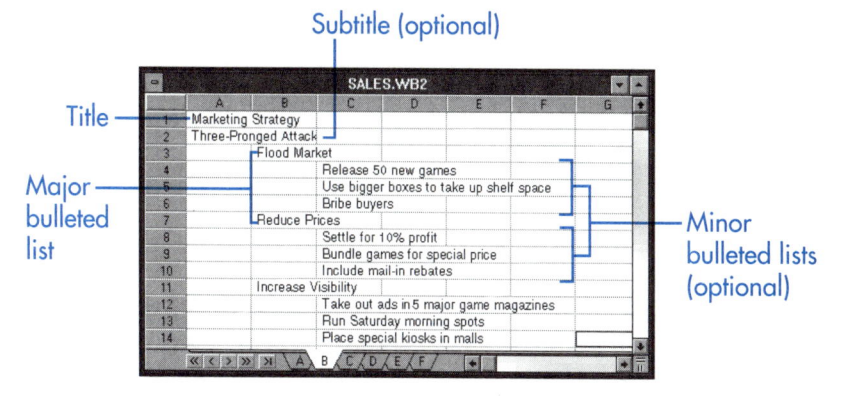

Figure 18.1 Type the data you want to transform into a bulleted list.

2. Drag over the entries you just typed.

3. Click on the Graph tool button.

4. Click where you want the upper left corner of the bullet chart to appear. Quattro Pro creates and inserts a black-and-white version of the chart.

5. Open the Graphics menu and select Graph Gallery. The Graph Gallery dialog box appears, presenting a list of professional designs for the bullet chart.

6. Click on the desired design in the Style list, then click on the OK button. Quattro Pro applies the design to the chart.

To modify any element on the chart (title, subtitle, major or minor bullet list), double-click on the chart, right-click on the element, select the Properties option, and enter your preferences. Click on the OK button when you're done.

> **Importing a Graphic** You can place a piece of clip art or other graphic on the chart by clicking on the Import button on the Graphics toolbar and selecting a graphic file. You can also draw on the chart, as explained in Lesson 17.

Creating a Slide Show

As you create graphs and bullet charts, Quattro Pro places an icon for each graph or chart on the objects page (the last page of the notebook). You can assemble these icons into an on-screen slide show by performing the following steps:

1. Click on the SpeedTab button to display the last notebook page.

2. Hold down the Shift key while clicking on the icon for each graph and chart you want to include in the slide show. Click on the icons in the order in which you want them displayed.

3. Click on the Create Slide Show button. A dialog box appears, prompting you to name the slide show.

4. Type a name for the slide show (up to 15 characters), and click on the OK button. Quattro Pro assembles the slides and displays them in the edit window, as shown in Figure 18.2.

Creating a Slide Show 103

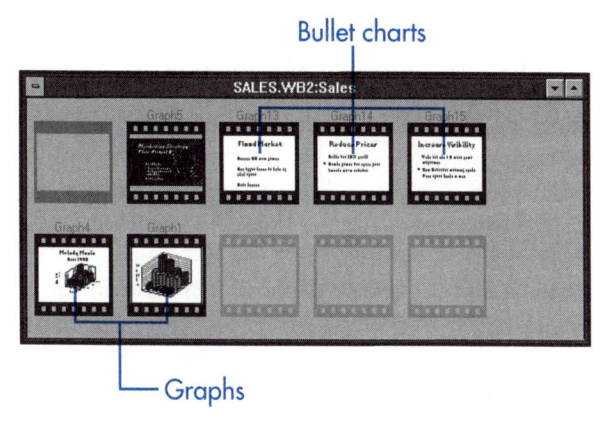

Figure 18.2 The edit slide show window.

You can display the slide show by clicking on the Run Slide Show button in the Toolbar. Press PgDn to view the next slide or PgUp to view the previous slide. You'll learn how to time the slides later in this lesson.

Using the Slide Show Expert

To create a slide show that consists mostly of bullet charts, use the Slide Show Expert to get started. Take the following steps:

1. Type the text for two or more bullet charts on a single notebook page. (See "Creating a Bullet Chart" earlier in this lesson.) The Slide Show Expert will be able to tell where each chart begins by a new entry in the Title column, or by a blank row between charts. The Slide Show Expert will display the charts in the order in which you type them.

2. Drag over the entries you just typed.

3. Click on the Experts button. The Experts dialog box appears.

4. Click on the Slide Show Expert button. The Slide Show Expert - Step 1 of 3 dialog box appears. The preview area shows the first bullet chart.

5. Click on the Next Step button. The Step 2 of 3 dialog box appears, prompting you to select a look for your chart.

6. Click on a master slide design in the list on the right, and then click on the Next Step button. The Step 3 of 3 dialog box appears, prompting you to type a name for the show.

7. Type a name for the slide show (up to 15 characters).

8. Click on From List, and select a transition effect from the list. The transition effect is an animated movement from one slide to the next.

9. Click on the Create Show button. The Slide Show Expert creates the slide show and displays it in an edit window.

Customizing Your Slide Show

The slide show's edit window lets you quickly rearrange the slides, select a transitional effect, and specify the time it takes to move from one slide to the next. To move a slide, simply drag it from its current location to its new location and release the mouse button. To pick a transitional effect or time, take the following steps:

1. Drag a selection box around all the slides. (You can also change transition effects and times for individual slides.)

2. Right-click on one of the slides, and click on Selected Objects Properties. The Selected Objects object inspector appears, as shown in Figure 18.3.

Creating a Slide Show   105

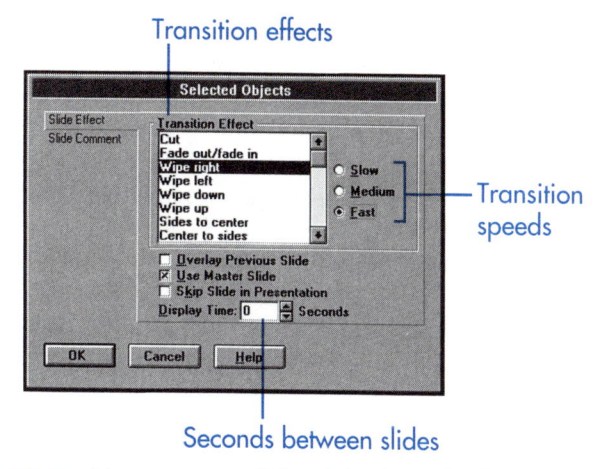

Figure 18.3 You can control the slide show display.

(Dialog box labeled "Selected Objects" with Transition effects list, Transition speeds (Slow, Medium, Fast), and Seconds between slides setting.)

3. Click on the desired transitional effect and then click on Slow, Medium, or Fast (to specify how fast you want the transition to proceed).

4. Click on the arrows to the right of the Display Time spin box to set the number of seconds between slides.

5. Click on the OK button.

Now, when you click on the Run Slide Show button, you can sit back and watch as Quattro Pro automatically moves from one slide to the next.

Printing a Slide Show

You can print a slide show on paper (or transparencies, if your printer has this capability). Here's what you do:

1. Drag a selection box around all the slides in the edit window.

2. Open the File menu and select Print.

3. Click on the Print button. Quattro Pro prints the selected slides.

In this lesson, you learned how to create a bullet chart, assemble charts and graphs into a slide show, display the slide show on-screen, and print a slide show. In the next lesson, you'll learn how to create a database for storing and managing information.

Lesson 19

Creating a Database

In this lesson, you'll learn how to create and save a database for storing and managing information electronically.

Understanding Database Basics

A *database* is a tool used for storing, organizing, and retrieving information. For example, if you wanted to save the names and addresses of all the people on your holiday-card list, you could create a database for storing the following information for each person: first name, last name, street number, and so on. Each piece of information is entered into a separate *field*. All of the fields for one person on the list make a *record*. In Quattro Pro, a cell is a field, and a row of field entries makes a record. Figure 19.1 illustrates the parts that make up a database.

Field names

	A	B	C	D	E	F	G
1							
2	RECORD#	FNAME	LNAME	ADDRESS	CITY	STATE	ZIP
3	3	Mary	Abolt	8517 Grandview Avenue	San Diego	CA	77987
4	11	Carey	Bistro	987 N. Cumbersome Lane	Detroit	MI	88687
5	13	Adrienne	Bullow	5643 N. Gaylord Ave.	Philadelphia	PA	27639
6	10	Chuck	Burger	6754 W. Lakeview Drive	Boston	MA	56784
7	7	Nicholas	Capetti	1345 W. Bilford Ave.	New Orleans	LA	12936
8	16	Gary	Davell	76490 E. Billview	New York	NY	76453
9	17	Kathy	Estrich	8763 W. Cloverdale Ave.	Paradise	TX	54812
10	4	Joseph	Fugal	2764 W. 56th Place	Chicago	IL	60678
11	12	Marie	Gabel	8764 N. Demetrius Blvd.	Miami	FL	88330
12	6	Lisa	Kasdan	8976 Westhaven Drive	Orlando	FL	88329
13	1	William	Kennedy	5567 Bluehill Circle	Indianapolis	IN	46224
14	2	Marion	Kraft	1313 Mockingbird Lane	Los Angeles	CA	77856
15	14	John	Kramden	5401 N. Randy	Pittsburgh	PA	27546

Each row is a record.   Each cell contains a field entry.

Figure 19.1 The parts of a database.

You must observe the following rules when you enter information into your database:

- **Field Names:** You must enter field names in the first row of the database; for example, type **First Name** for first name, **Last Name** for the last name. Do *not* skip a row between the field names row and the first record.

- **Records:** Each record must be in a separate row, with no empty rows between records. The cells in a given column must contain information of the same type. For example, if you have a ZIP CODE column, all cells in that column must contain a ZIP code. You can create a *calculated field*—one that uses information from another field of the same record and produces a result. To do so, enter a formula, as explained in Lesson 4.

> **Record Numbering** It's a good idea to add a column that numbers the records. If the records are sorted incorrectly, you can use the numbered column to restore the records to their original order.

Creating a Database

To create a database, enter data into the cells as you would enter data on any spreadsheet page. As you enter data, follow these guidelines:

- You must enter field names in the top row of the database. Field names can be up to 16 characters long, with no blank spaces at the beginning or end.

- Type field entries into each cell to create a record. (You can leave a field blank, but you may run into problems later when you sort the database.)

Creating a Database

- Do *not* leave an empty row between the field names and the records or between any records.

- If you want to enter street numbers with the street names, start the entry with an apostrophe so that Quattro Pro interprets the entry as text instead of as a value.

- Keep the records on one page. You cannot have a database that spans several pages.

In earlier versions of Quattro Pro, you had to select the data you entered and then enter a command to define the database. In version 6.0, you simply type the data. Whenever you enter a database command, Quattro Pro "knows" that you want to treat the entries as a database rather than as spreadsheet data.

Adding Records

The easiest way to add records to your database is to type the records at the end of the current list. You can also have Quattro Pro create a data entry form for the database. To create such a form, perform the following steps:

1. Drag over all the cells that make up the database, including the field names and all the records. (To start a new database, type only a row of field names, then drag over the field names and one row of blank cells below the field names.)

2. Open the Tools menu, select Database Tools, and select Form. The Database Form dialog box appears, prompting you to specify the range of cells that make up your database (which you already did in step 1).

3. Click on the OK button. Quattro Pro creates a data entry form using the field names you entered. Figure 19.2 shows a sample form.

Lesson 19

Field names — Record

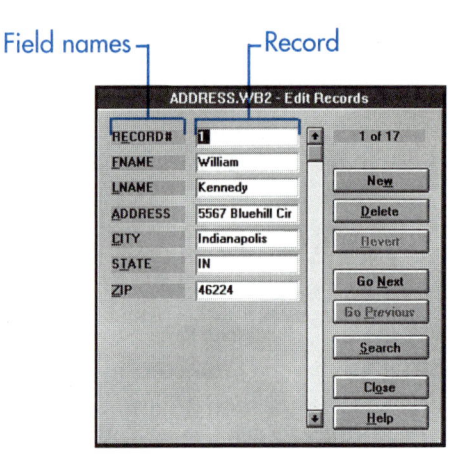

Figure 19.2 Sample data entry form for a database.

4. To enter a new record, click on the New button and then type your entries in the field name text boxes. Press Tab to move from one text box to the next; press Shift+Tab to move back.

One problem with database forms is that you cannot save a form. You must perform these same steps again to enter additional records.

The Form dialog box has a scroll bar that you can use to flip through the records. In Lesson 20, you will learn some more advanced tools for finding records.

Saving the Database

After you've entered your data, you should save the database as you would save a notebook. Refer to Lesson 6 for details.

In this lesson, you learned how to create a basic database. In the next lesson, you will learn how to search and sort a database.

Lesson 20

Sorting and Searching a Database

In this lesson, you will learn how to sort the records in a database and locate specific records.

Sorting a Database

You can enter records in any order. You can then use the Sort feature to sort the records in various ways. For example, you can sort the records numerically in ascending order by ZIP code, or alphabetically in descending order by last name.

The sorting instructions you give Quattro Pro are referred to as *sort keys*. The sort key tells Quattro Pro which column to sort on and whether to sort in *ascending order* (1,2,3... or A,B,C...) or *descending order* (10,9,8... or Z,Y,X...). You can use more than one sort key to sort your records. For example, you can sort records first by ZIP code and then by last name. Quattro Pro would sort the records numerically by ZIP code; any records having the same ZIP code entry would then be sorted by last name.

Common Sorting Error When you sort a database, the most important thing to remember is to *exclude the top row*—the one with the field names—from the block of cells you want to sort. If you include the top row, it will be sorted along with the other rows; the field name row may not end up at the top of the database.

Lesson 20

To sort a database, perform the following steps:

1. Select the records you want to sort. (Don't include the field names.)

2. Open the Block menu and select Sort. The Block Sort dialog box appears, as shown in Figure 20.1. The selected range of cells is shown in the Block text box.

Block that will be sorted

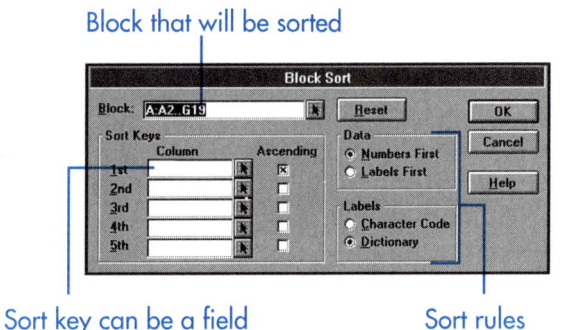

```
                    Block Sort
Block: A:A2..G19           Reset          OK
Sort Keys                  Data           Cancel
       Column    Ascending  ● Numbers First
  1st                 X     ○ Labels First  Help
  2nd
  3rd                       Labels
  4th                       ○ Character Code
  5th                       ● Dictionary
```

Sort key can be a field   Sort rules
name or cell address.

Figure 20.1 The Block Sort dialog box.

3. Click inside the 1st Sort Keys text box, and click on the Point button. Quattro Pro returns you to the spreadsheet so you can select the first column you want to sort on.

> **Named Fields** A quick way to specify which field you want to sort on is to type the field name in the 1st text box. You must type the field name exactly as it appears in the database.

4. Click in any cell in the column you want to sort the records by, and click on the Maximize button in the Block Sort title bar.

5. Make sure there is an X in the Ascending text box to sort in ascending order, or click on Ascending to remove the X and sort in descending order.

6. To enter another sort key, repeat steps 3-5 for the 2nd Sort Key text box. (You can use up to 5 sort keys.)

7. In the Data area, select Numbers First if you want records that contain numbers to be positioned at the top of the list. Select Labels First to have text entries appear first.

8. In the Labels area, select Character Code to sort all uppercase letters first (BB comes before aa, and so on), or select Dictionary to ignore case (for example Aa is before BB).

9. Click on the OK button. Quattro Pro sorts the records accordingly.

Searching for Records

Quattro Pro provides two ways to locate records in a database. You can use a *search form* (which is easy) or use a *criteria table* (which is a bit more difficult). Regardless of which method you use, you must enter *search criteria* to tell Quattro Pro which records to find. Search criteria can be as simple as a field entry "Smith" or complex as a conditional entry ">$450" (greater than $450). Table 20.1 shows the conditional operators you can use.

Table 20.1 Conditional Operators

Operator	Meaning
=	Equal to
>	Greater than

continues

Table 20.1 Continued

Operator	Meaning
<	Less than
>=	Greater than or equal to
<=	Less than or equal to
<>	Not equal to

You can also use the following *wildcard* characters when specifying criteria:

?   Represents a single character

*   Represents multiple characters

~   Represents any character *except* this one

For example, in the Name field, you could type **M*** to find everyone whose name begins with an *M*. To find everyone whose three-digit department code has *10* as the last two digits, you could type **?10**.

Using a Form to Search for Records

The easiest way to search for records is to use a database form. Follow these steps:

1. Select the database you want to search, including the field name row.

2. Open the Tools menu, select Database Tools, and select Form. The Database Form dialog box appears, prompting you to specify the range of cells that make up your database (which you already did in step 1).

Sorting and Searching a Database 115

3. Click on the OK button. Quattro Pro displays a data form showing the first record in the database.

4. Click on the Search button. A blank Search Records form appears.

5. Type the criteria you would like to use in the appropriate fields (see Figure 20.2). Use only the fields you want to search. For example, if you want to find all Bostonians whose last names start with K, you could type **Boston** in the CITY field and **K*** in the LNAME field.

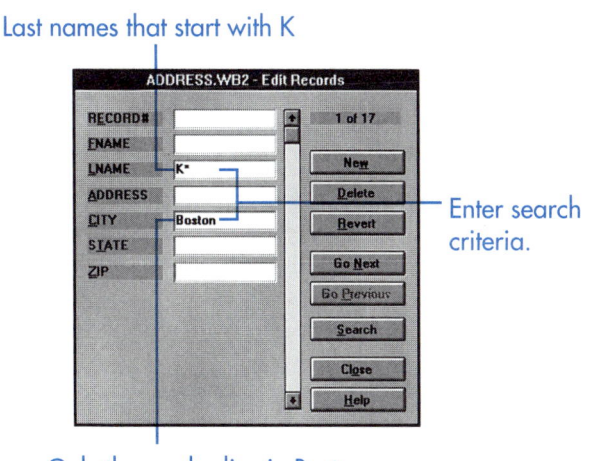

Last names that start with K

Enter search criteria.

Only those who live in Boston

Figure 20.2 Use the Search Records form to find records.

6. Click on the Go Next button to view the first record that matches your search criteria.

7. Click on the Go Next or Go Previous button to display the next or previous record.

8. When you are done reviewing records, click on the Close button.

Searching with a Criteria Table

Another way to have Quattro Pro search for records is to create a *criteria table*. A criteria table consists of the field names you want to search and the criteria you want to search for. Optionally, you can specify a destination (*output block*) to which Quattro Pro can extract the records it finds. Take the following steps:

1. Copy the field names from the top row of the database to a blank row below the last record. (Tip: leave at least two blank rows between the last record and this row.)

2. **(Optional)** Enter the label **CRITERIA** in the row above the copied row, to indicate the purpose of this table.

3. In the cells below the criteria table field names, type your search criteria. For example, under LNAME, you might type **K***. (You don't need to type an entry in every field.) See Figure 20.3.

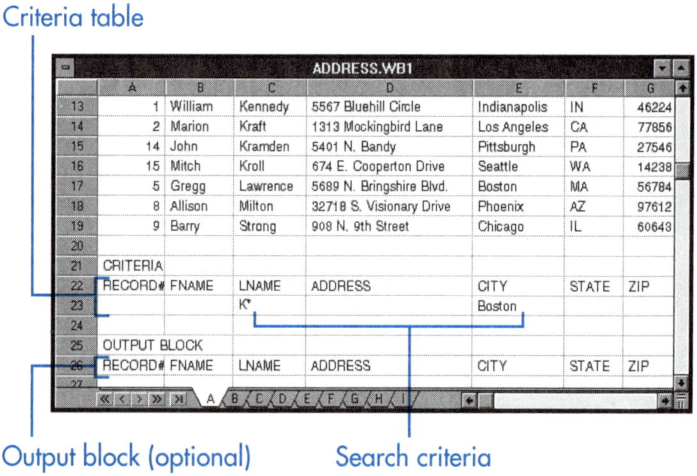

Criteria table

Output block (optional)   Search criteria

Figure 20.3 A criteria table can locate records or copy them to an output block.

Sorting and Searching a Database

4. **(Optional)** Create a place for an output block by copying the field names from the top row of the database to a blank row below the criteria table. Leave two blank rows between the criteria table and this row.

> **Limit Output Data** To extract only specific information (for example, the last name and state), delete all field names except for the names whose data you want to extract.

5. **(Optional)** Enter the label **OUTPUT BLOCK** in the row above the copied row, to indicate the purpose of this table. (See Figure 20.3.)

6. Select the records you want to search. (Be sure to include the field names!)

7. Open the Tools menu, select Database Tools, and select Query. The Data Query dialog box appears. The range of selected cells appears in the Database Block text box.

8. Click on the Criteria Table Point button, drag over the field names and search criteria in the criteria table, and click on the Maximize button in the Data Query title bar.

9. If you included an output block, click on the Output Block Point button, drag over the field names for the output block, and click on the Maximize button in the Data Query title bar.

10. Click on one of the following buttons:

> **Locate** finds the first record that matches the search criteria and highlights it. You can use the ↓ key to go to the next record. Press Esc when you are done.
>
> **Extract** copies all records that match the search criteria to the output table, essentially creating a subset of the original database.

In this lesson, you learned how to sort and search a database. In the next lesson, you will learn how to use some tools for handling home finances.

Lesson 21

Using the Home Finance Tools

In this lesson, you will learn how to create budget, loan amortization, and refinance spreadsheets without having to enter formulas or functions.

Using the Budget Expert

Although you can create your own budget notebook by typing entries and formulas into cells, Quattro Pro's Budget Expert can help you get started. This tool leads you through a nine step process for entering income and expense categories and formatting the result. To use the Budget Expert, perform the following steps:

1. Click on the New Notebook icon. Quattro Pro opens a new notebook window for your budget.

2. Click on the Experts button. The Experts dialog box appears.

3. Click on Budget Expert. The Budget Expert - Step 1 of 9 dialog box appears.

4. Click on the Budget Tool you want to use. When you click on a tool, a description of it appears on the left. (For this example, click on Home-Actual vs. Plan.)

5. Click on the Next Step button. A list of income items appears, as shown in Figure 21.1.

Lesson 21

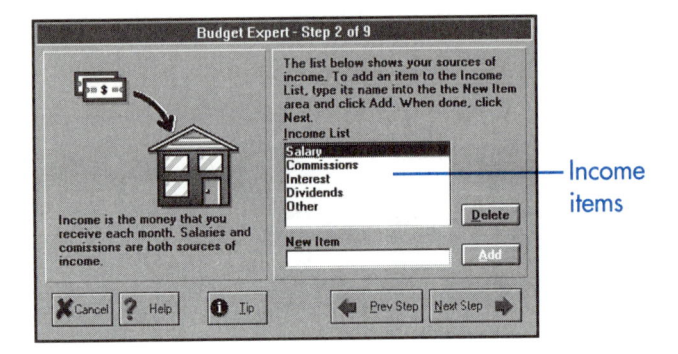

Figure 21.1 You can add or delete income items.

6. Delete any items in the Income List that do not apply to you. (Click on the item, and then click the Delete button.)

7. To add items to the Income List, click inside the New Item text box, type an income item, and click on Add.

> **Two Salaries?** If you have two salary incomes, delete the Salary item, and add two distinct salary items—for example, **Joe's Salary** and **Mary's Salary**.

8. Click on the Next Step button.

9. Delete any items in the Expense List that do not apply to you. (Click on the item, and then click the Delete button.)

10. To add items to the Expense List, click inside the New Item text box, type an income item, and click on Add.

11. Click on the Next Step button.

Using the Home Finance Tools 121

12. Proceed through the remaining dialog boxes to enter your formatting preferences for the budget sheet. Click on the Next Step button to proceed to the next dialog box. When you come to the last dialog box, the Next Step button becomes the Build Budget button.

13. Click on the Build Budget button. Quattro Pro creates the budget spreadsheet, as shown in Figure 21.2.

14. Enter your budget data in the spreadsheet.

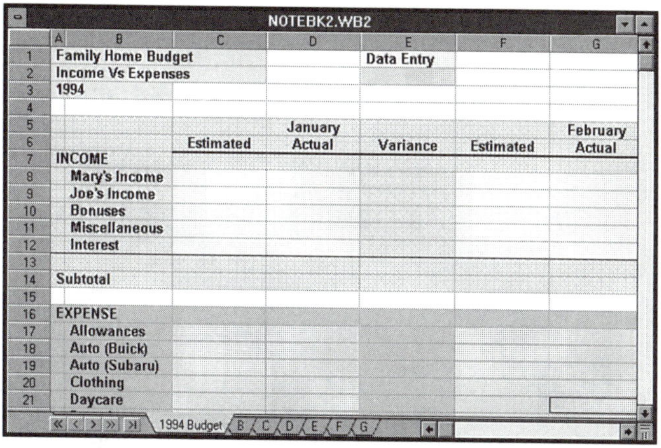

Figure 21.2 The budget spreadsheet can compare actual spending against your goals.

The budget spreadsheet may or may not be detailed enough for your use. For example, there's only one cell per month for a Groceries entry, so you must tally your grocery bills and then type in a total. You may want to create a separate page for Groceries (and other such categories), and insert a formula in the budget spreadsheet that inserts the total from the Groceries page.

Refinancing a Loan

If interest rates ever start declining again, you may consider refinancing your mortgage. When the need arises, you can use Quattro Pro's Refinance tool:

1. Click on the Experts button. The Experts dialog box appears.

2. Click on the Analysis Expert. The Analysis Tools Expert dialog box appears, listing financial and statistical tools.

3. Click on Mortgage Refinancing at the bottom of the list, and click on the Next Step button. The Mortgage Refinancing options appear on the right. (Figure 21.3 shows options with sample entries.)

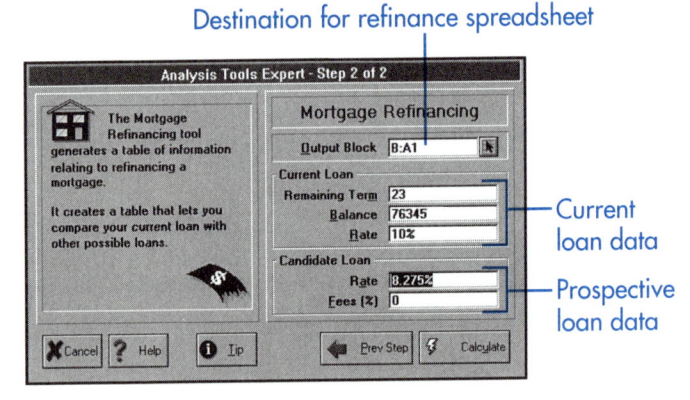

Figure 21.3 You can quickly determine whether refinancing will save you money.

4. Click on the Output Block Point button, and click on a cell in a blank area or blank page of the current notebook. (You don't want to copy the refinance spreadsheet over existing data.)

5. In the Current Loan area, type the following entries:

Using the Home Finance Tools

Remaining Term: The number of years you still must pay on the loan. The field accepts only whole years, but you will be able to enter a fraction of a year in the spreadsheet.

Balance: How much you still owe on the loan.

Rate: The current interest rate. Be sure to type the percent sign (**%**) or type the percent as a decimal: **.09** or **9%**, not just 9.

6. In the Candidate Loan area, type the following entries:

Rate: The prospective refinance interest rate. Be sure to type the percent sign (**%**) or type the percent as a decimal: **.09** or **9%**, not just 9.

Fees (%): The number of points (if any) you must pay to refinance.

Changing the Term Although you can't change the term in the dialog box (for example, to change from a 30- to a 15-year loan), you will be able to experiment with terms in the spreadsheet Quattro Pro creates.

7. Click on the Calculate button. Quattro Pro creates a refinance spreadsheet. Scroll to the right to see how much refinancing saves (or costs) you. (For a description of the items that make up the sheet, repeat steps 1 through 3, and then click on the Help button.)

You're not done yet. Now, you can fine-tune the refinance spreadsheet by entering fractions of years and changing the term of the loan.

Lesson 21

If you want to know how much you will save (or lose) over the life of the loan, you can further customize the spreadsheet by adding the following three formulas (see Figure 21.4):

Loan Life (Current): This formula multiplies the remaining term (in years) by 12 (months) times the monthly payment. The result shows how much you will end up paying for your house with the current loan.

Loan Life (Candidate): This formula multiplies the new term (in years) by 12 (months) times the monthly payment. The result shows how much you will end up paying for your house with the new loan.

Total Savings: This formula subtracts the Candidate Loan Life result from the Current Loan Life result to show the total amount you will save (or lose) by refinancing.

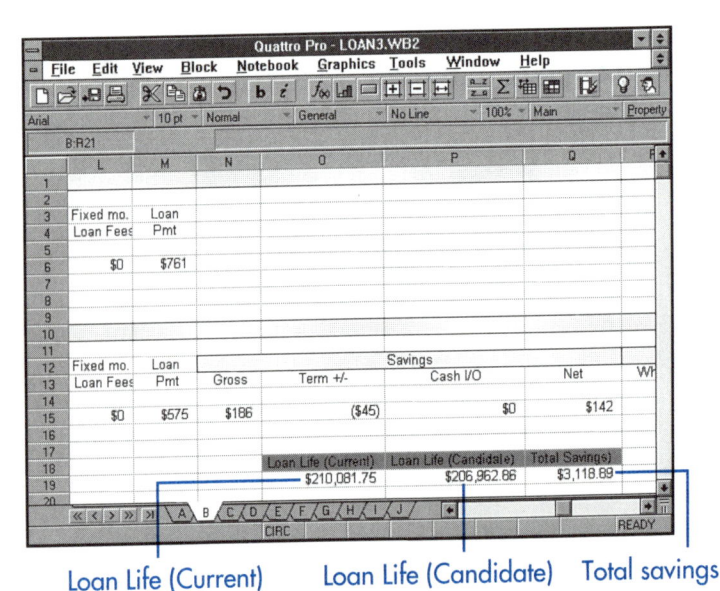

Figure 21.4 Customize the spreadsheet to determine total saved (or lost).

Creating an Amortization Schedule

Amortization schedules are useful for determining how much of each loan payment is going for interest, and how much is paying off the principal. In the past, you had to go through an accountant or loan officer to get this information. With Quattro Pro, you can do it yourself:

1. Click on the Experts button. The Experts dialog box appears.

2. Click on the Analysis Expert. The Analysis Tool Expert - Step 1 dialog box appears.

3. Click on Amortization Schedule, and click on the Next Step button. The Amortization Schedule options appear on the right. (Figure 21.5 shows options with sample entries.)

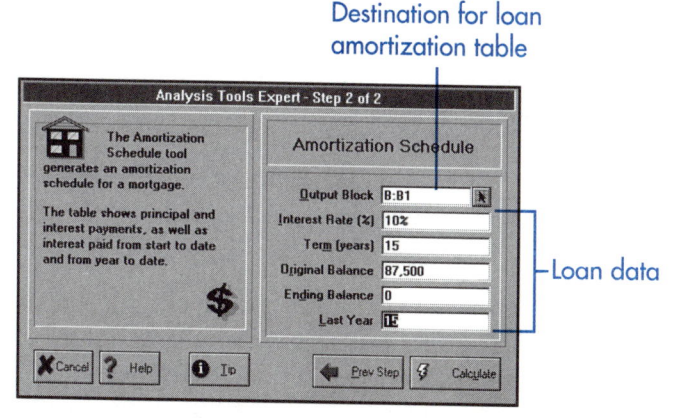

Figure 21.5 Enter the loan data, and Quattro Pro creates the table.

4. Click on the Output Block Point button, and click on a cell in a blank area or blank page of the current notebook.

Lesson 21

5. Type your loan data in the following text boxes:

> **Interest Rate (%):** The annual interest rate for the loan. Be sure to type the percent sign **(%)** or type the percent as a decimal: **.09** or **9%**, not just 9.
>
> **Term:** The total number of years, *not* the number of years remaining.
>
> **Original Balance:** The total amount you borrowed.
>
> **Ending Balance:** Usually 0, because your last payment will pay off the loan. If you have a lump sum (*balloon*) payment at the end of the loan, enter the amount here.
>
> **Last Year:** The last year for which you want amortization data. For example, you may have a 30-year loan, but you want data for only the first 10 years.

6. Click on the Calculate button. Quattro Pro creates the amortization schedule, and inserts it in the output block.

The schedule determines January 1, 2001 as the first payment date. To change the date, click inside the cell under 1st PMT, and click on the Formula Composer button (the button with **fx** on it). Replace the **101** in the Year text box with the year of the first payment (for example, **95**), and replace the month with the first payment month (for example, **3** for March). Click on the ✓ button.

Paying Extra Principal You can pay off a loan early by paying extra toward the principal each month. Type an entry in the cell directly below Extra Prin (for example, type **50**). Scroll down to see how many years early you will have paid off the loan. Of course, if your loan has an early-payment penalty, paying off the loan early may not be the most financially sound option.

In this lesson, you learned how to use Quattro Pro's financial tools to quickly create specialized financial spreadsheets. In the next lesson, you will learn how to analyze data using data models.

Lesson 22

Analyzing Data with Data Models

In this lesson, you will learn how to rearrange and summarize data to create reports.

Quattro Pro features a Data Modeling Desktop that allows you to rearrange the columns and rows of a spreadsheet quickly to summarize data and lay it out in a meaningful format.

Suppose you're a toy manufacturer, and you have a spreadsheet that tracks the sales of four popular toys through two major outlets. You can create a report that shows which outlet has the greatest total sales. You can then rearrange the data to show which store sells the most of each toy. Figure 22.1 illustrates how a crosstab report works.

> **Plain English**
>
> **Crosstab Report** A crosstab report is a tool that lets you experiment with the relationships between different data sets by dragging spreadsheet data around; for example, you can look at sales by salesperson or by region. A crosstab report consists of three basic elements: top label bars, side label bars, and data. You rearrange data by dragging the label bars.

Analyzing Data with Data Models   129

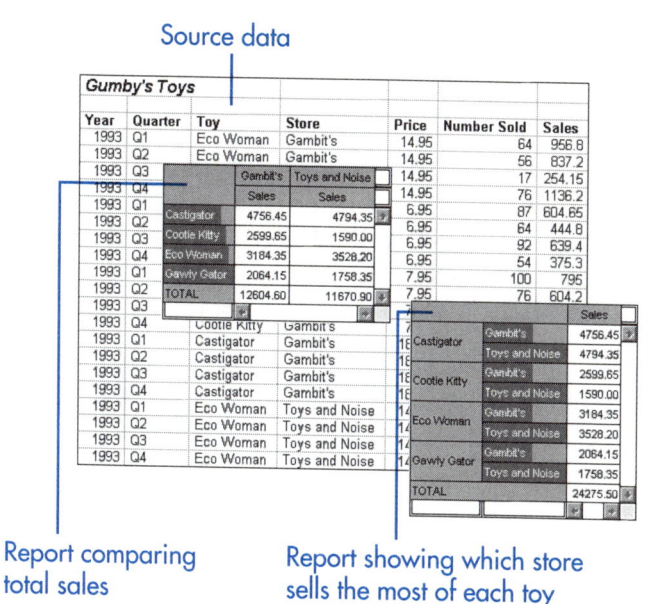

Figure 22.1 A crosstab report summarizes and organizes your data.

Source data, *Report comparing total sales*, *Report showing which store sells the most of each toy*

Opening a New Report

The first step in creating a crosstab report is to transfer your spreadsheet data to the Data Modeling Desktop. Perform the following steps:

1. Open the notebook that contains the data you want to use.

2. Drag over the data you want to include in the report (include all column and row labels in the selection).

3. Open the Tools menu and select Data Modeling Desktop. The Send Data to Data Modeling Desktop dialog box appears, prompting you to select the source data (which you did in step 2) and a destination for the data (the first blank page in the current notebook, by default).

Lesson 22

4. To have the data sent elsewhere, tab to the Cell for Returned Data box, and type the desired page and cell address.

5. To have Quattro Pro automatically update your report whenever you change data in the source spreadsheet, click on Hot for the Data Exchange Method. If you leave the setting at Cold, you will need to paste updated data into the report.

6. Click on the OK button. Quattro Pro extracts the marked data, runs the Modeling Desktop, and places the data in the source window, as shown in Figure 22.2.

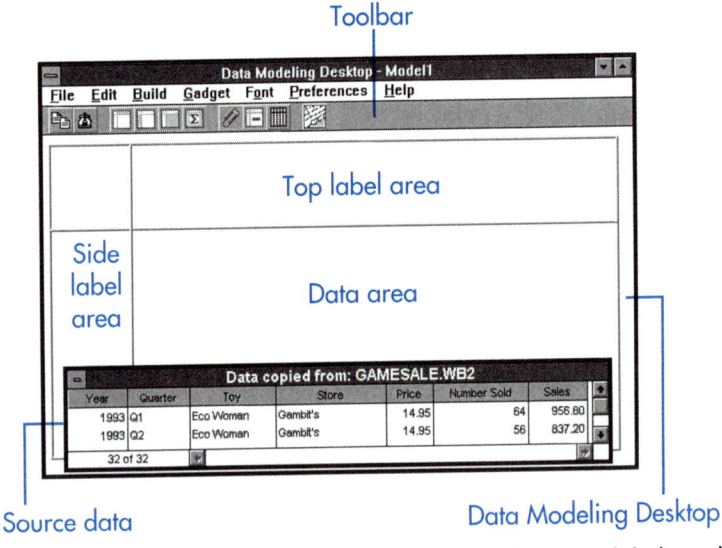

Figure 22.2 You will create a report by dragging labels and data from the source window to the Data Modeling Desktop.

Analyzing Data with Data Models 131

Building a Crosstab Report

Once the source data is on the Desktop, you can use it to create the top and side label bars and to add data to the report. Take the following steps:

1. Click on a column in the source window, hold down the mouse button, and drag the column to the top or side label bar area on the Desktop. For example, to determine how many toys each store sold, drag the Store column to the top label area, and drag the Toy column to the side label area.

   Adding Multiple Labels To add more than one label, shift+click on each column you want to add, and then click on the Top Label Bar or Side Label Bar button:

   Top ▭▭ Side

2. Repeat step 1 to place additional labels on the Desktop. You can use each label only once.

3. Click on the column of data you want to add to the report, hold down the mouse button, and drag the column to the data area.

You can repeat these steps to place additional labels and data into your report. Your table will start to take on a form, as shown in Figure 22.3.

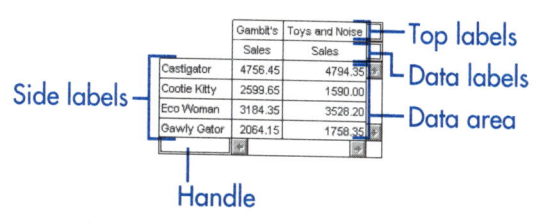

	Gambit's	Toys and Noise
	Sales	Sales
Castigator	4756.45	4794.35
Cootie Kitty	2599.65	1590.00
Eco Woman	3184.35	3528.20
Gawly Gator	2064.15	1758.35

Side labels · Top labels · Data labels · Data area · Handle

Figure 22.3 A sample crosstab report.

Lesson 22

Rearranging Your Data

Once you have a basic report on-screen, you can rearrange the data to view it in different ways. The following list explains the options you have for restructuring the report:

Remove a Label Bar: To remove a label bar (and its data) from the report, click on the handle for that label (the white box at the right end of a top label bar or at the bottom of a side label bar). Then, click on the Remove button.

Change Label Bar Levels: If you have two or more top labels, you can rearrange them by dragging one up or down. You can rearrange side labels by dragging them left or right.

Pivot Label Bars: You can quickly rearrange data by dragging label bars to different areas of the desktop. For example, you can move a side label bar to the top or to the data area. To pivot a label bar, move the mouse pointer over its handle, hold down the mouse button, and drag the handle to where you want the labels placed. (See Figure 22.4.)

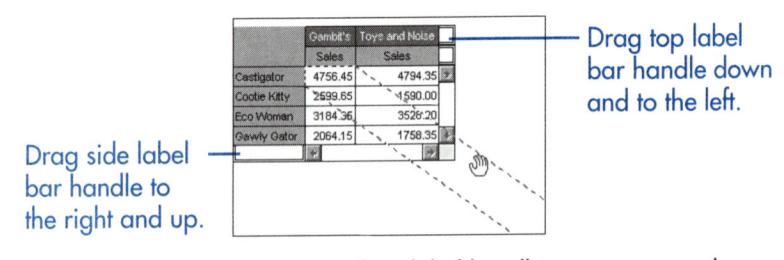

Drag side label bar handle to the right and up.

Drag top label bar handle down and to the left.

Figure 22.4 You can drag label handles to rearrange data.

Analyzing Data with Data Models   133

Creating Totals

In reports, you will often find it useful to total rows or columns of data. To create totals, perform the following steps:

1. Click on the handle of the label for which you want to create a total.

2. Click on the Sum button. Quattro Pro totals the data, and inserts a Total row or column.

Using the Data Modeling Gadgets

The Data Modeling Desktop contains several tools, called *Gadgets*, that you can use to quickly format reports. To use a Gadget, select the item you want to format and then right-click on it. You can also open the Gadget menu and select the desired Gadget:

Display: Allows you to change the report's grid lines. You can display horizontal or vertical grid lines or a crisscross pattern.

Format: Lets you pick a numerical format for your data. For example, you can display it as a percent or dollar amount.

Formula: Allows you to specify which formula you want to use in a Total column (a column you created with the Sum button). For example, you can choose Average or Percent instead of Sum.

Limit: Lets you restrict some data from being included in a report. When the Limit Gadget is displayed, click on the column in the source window that contains the data you want to limit. You can then specify the range of data you want to include.

Name: Allows you to change a label name in the report.

Changing the Font Size

You can change the font size for labels and values by selecting the text, opening the Font menu, and clicking on a font size. For more control over the appearance of a report, copy the report to a notebook (as explained in the next section) and use the formatting tools, as explained in Lessons 10 through 12.

Copying the Report to a Notebook

If you want the copied report updated whenever you change data in the source spreadsheet, you can set the copy options to create a *hot link*. To set the copy options, open the Preferences menu and select Copy to Quattro Pro Options. In the dialog box that appears, select the Always hot link option (or enter other preferences), and then click on the OK button.

When you are done creating a report, you can copy it back to your notebook by clicking on the Copy to Quattro Pro button.

In this lesson, you learned how to create crosstab reports, rearrange data, and format a report. In the next lesson, you'll learn how to use another data analysis tool: scenarios.

Lesson 23

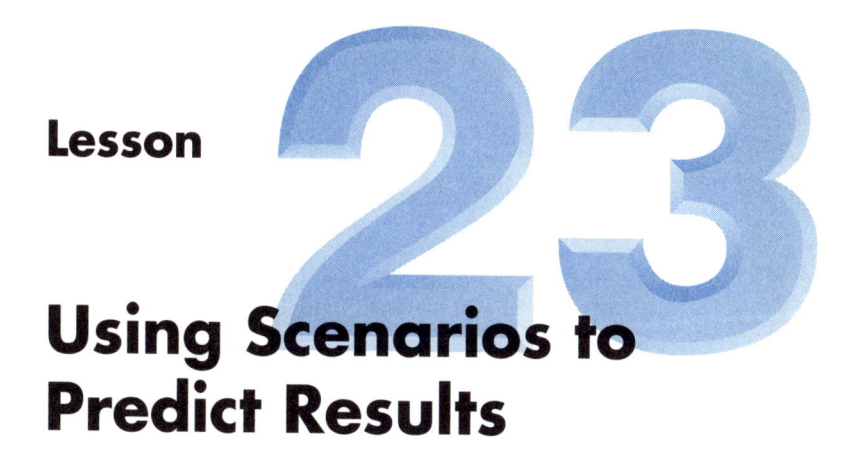

Using Scenarios to Predict Results

In this lesson, you will learn how to use scenarios to determine a worst-case and best-case outcome.

What Are Scenarios?

Scenarios are sets of values that you plug into an equation to determine how different values affect the results. Say you have a spreadsheet, like the one in Figure 23.1, that determines a monthly mortgage payment based on the following variables: principal (money borrowed), interest rate, and term (number of payment periods). You can create scenarios that plug in different values for the variables and determine the monthly payment for each set of values. One scenario might determine, for example, the monthly payment for a $100,000 loan at 8.9% over 30 years. Another might determine the payment for a $120,000 loan at 8.5% over 15 years.

To create scenarios, you must first decide which spreadsheet cells are to contain the data you want to experiment with. These cells are called the *changing cells*. You must also decide which cell(s) will contain the results of the changes: the *result cell(s)*. The scenarios you create will insert different sets of values into the changing cells and insert the outcomes into the result cell(s).

Lesson 23

Loan Calculation Worksheet	
Principal	$100,000.00
Annual Interest Rate	9.0000
Monthly Interest Rate	0.0075
Payment Periods	360
Payment Amount	
Total Paid	
Date of Loan	
Future Value	

— Spreadsheet for calculating monthly payments

Scenarios	Result Cells	
	Cells	Values
100K @9% 15-year	Payment Amount	$1,014.27
	Total Paid	$182,567.99
100K @9% 10-year	Payment Amount	$1,266.76
	Total Paid	$152,010.93
120K @9% 30-year	Payment Amount	$965.55
	Total Paid	$347,596.97
120K @9% 15-year	Payment Amount	$1,217.12
	Total Paid	$219,081.58
120K @9% 10-year	Payment Amount	$1,520.11
	Total Paid	$182,413.11

Scenarios

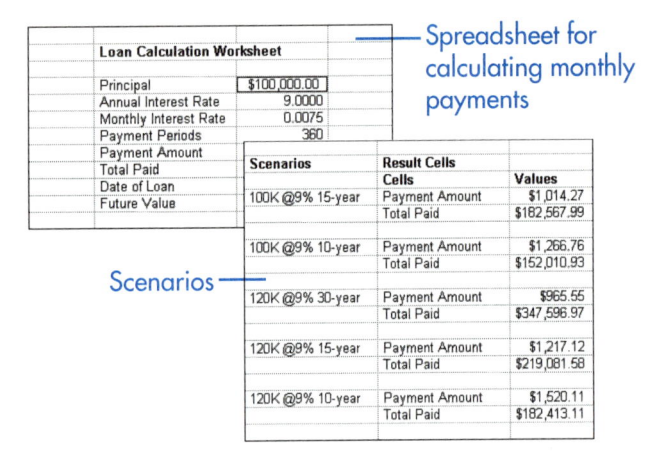

Figure 23.1 Scenarios help compare different situations.

Name the Changing and Result Cells
Before you create scenarios, name each changing and result cell (see Lesson 7). When you create scenarios, these names will appear above the corresponding values, making it easier to read the scenarios. If you don't name the cells, Quattro Pro displays only cell addresses.

Creating Scenarios with Scenario Expert

Quattro Pro's Scenario Expert leads you, step by step, through the process of creating scenarios. To use Scenario Expert, take the following steps:

1. Open the notebook that contains the data you want to use.

2. Click on the Experts button. The Experts dialog box appears.

Using Scenarios to Predict Results   137

3. Click on Scenario Expert. The Scenario Expert - Step 1 of 4 dialog box appears, prompting you to select the changing cells. (See Figure 23.2.)

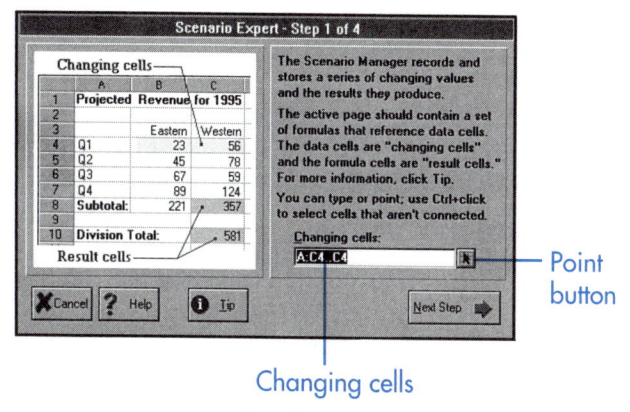

Figure 23.2 You must select the changing cells.

4. Click on the Point button, click on the first changing cell, and then Ctrl+click on each additional changing cell.

5. Click on the Maximize button in the Scenario Expert title bar, and click on the Next Step button. The Step 2 of 4 dialog box appears, prompting you to create a scenario.

6. Type a name for the scenario (up to 15 characters).

7. Change one or more of the values in the Changing cells and their values list.

8. Click on the Add Scenario button.

9. Repeat steps 5 through 7 to create additional scenarios.

10. Click on the Next Step button. The Step 3 of 4 dialog box appears, enabling you to view the results of the various scenarios.

11. **(Optional)** Select a scenario from the list, click on the Show Scenario button, and drag the dialog box title bar, so you can see the results in your spreadsheet. Changing values are highlighted in yellow. Result values are highlighted in green.

12. Click on the Next Step button, and click on the Create Report button. Scenario Expert calculates the results of all the scenarios and creates a Scenarios report page in the notebook. (See Figure 23.3.)

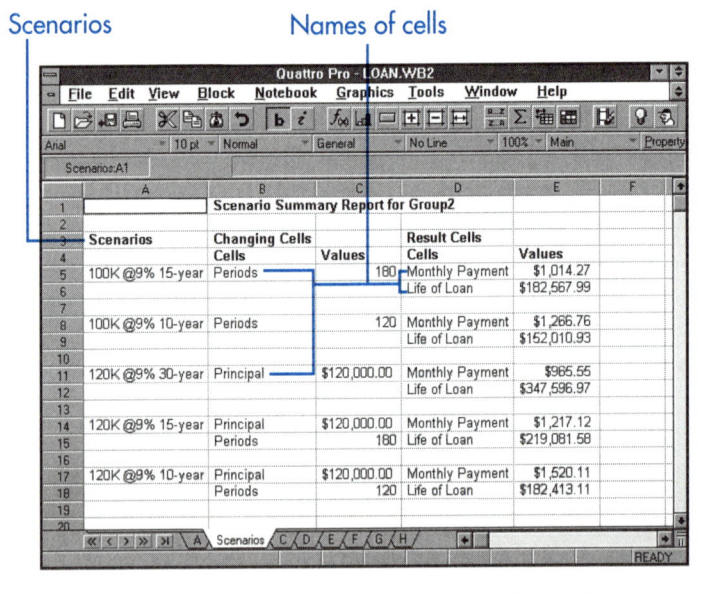

Figure 23.3 Scenario Expert creates a Scenarios report page.

Using the Scenario Manager

Once you have created scenarios, you can display, edit, or delete them using the Scenario Manager. Here's what you do:

Using Scenarios to Predict Results 139

1. Display the notebook page that contains the source data.

2. Open the Tools menu and select Scenario Manager. The Scenario Manager dialog box appears, as shown in Figure 23.4.

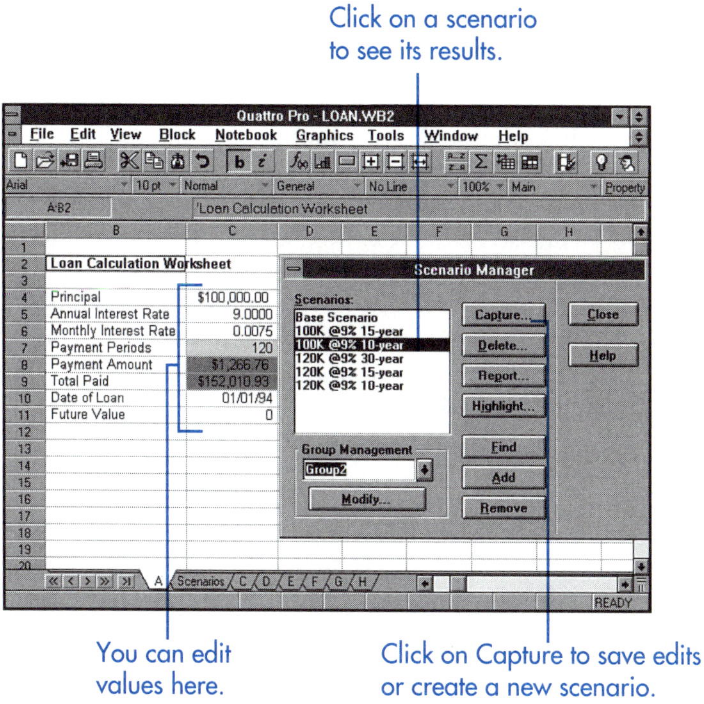

Click on a scenario to see its results.

You can edit values here.

Click on Capture to save edits or create a new scenario.

Figure 23.4 Use Scenario Manager to view, edit, and create scenarios.

3. To view a scenario's results, click on its name in the Scenarios list. (If the dialog box is in the way, drag the title bar to move it.)

4. Perform the following steps to edit a scenario:

   Enter your changes in the spreadsheet.

   Click on the Capture button, and then click on OK in the dialog box that appears.

5. Do the following to create a new scenario:

   Type an entry into at least one changing cell.

   Click on the Capture button.

   In the dialog box that appears, type a name in the Scenario Name text box, and then click on the OK button.

6. To update the Scenario Report you created earlier, click on the Report button, enter your preferences, and click on OK.

7. Click on the Close button when you are done.

In this lesson, you learned how to use scenarios to compare the results of different values. In the next lesson, you will learn how to automate your work with macros.

Lesson 24

Automating Your Work with Macros

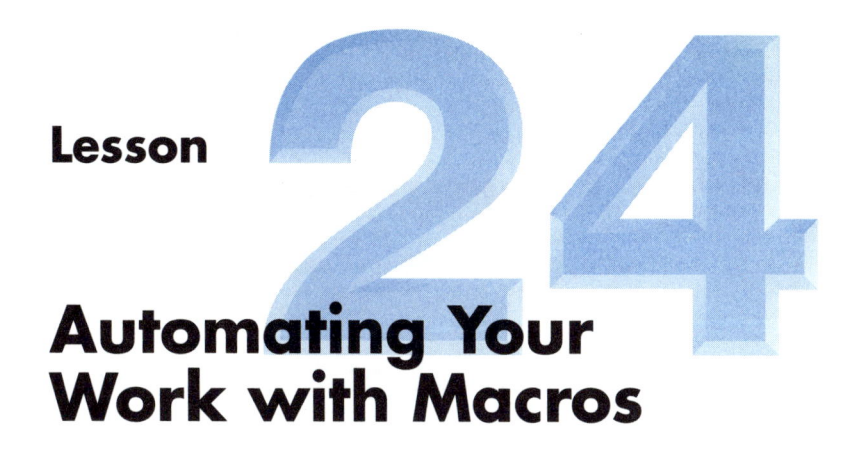

In this lesson, you will learn how to record commands and keystrokes and play them back.

What Is a Macro?

A *macro* is a collection of recorded keystrokes or menu selections that you can play back simply by pressing a key combination or selecting the macro from a menu. You can record dozens of keystrokes in a macro and play them back simply by pressing two keys. In this lesson, you will learn how to record and play macros.

Recording a Macro

Although you can create a macro by typing commands, it is far easier to have Quattro Pro record the macro. Take the following steps:

1. Open the Tools menu and select Macro. The Macro submenu appears.

2. Select Record. The Record Macro dialog box appears, as shown in Figure 24.1, prompting you to select an area of the spreadsheet in which to store macro commands.

Lesson 24

Point button

[Record Macro dialog box]

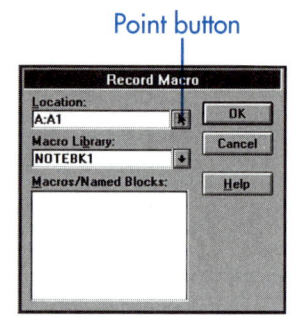

Figure 24.1 Quattro Pro stores the macro commands in a spreadsheet.

3. Click on the Location Point button, and then click on a blank cell that has no entries below it.

> **Don't Copy Macro Over Existing Data**
> Quattro Pro records macro commands into the current cell and the cells below it. If there are data in these cells, the macro commands will replace the data. Also, choose only *one* cell. If you choose a block that is too small, Quattro Pro might stop recording before the macro is complete.

4. Click on the Maximize button in the Record Macro title bar.

5. Click on the OK button. The dialog box disappears, and **REC** appears in the status line, indicating that Quattro Pro is ready to record your commands.

6. Perform the task whose steps you want to record. Quattro Pro records the steps as you perform them.

7. Open the Tools menu, select Macro, and select Stop Record. Quattro Pro stores the recorded macro in the specified block.

Automating Your Work with Macros

8. Right-click inside the first macro cell and select Names. The Block Names dialog box appears.

9. Type a name for the macro, and then click on the Add button. The name is inserted into the list of block names.

10. Click on the Close button. The macro is added to the macro list, and the Block Names dialog box disappears.

You can assign a shortcut key combination, such as Ctrl+A, to a macro. When naming the macro block, type a backslash followed by any letter of the alphabet (A through Z). For example, type **A** to use Ctrl+A to run the macro. Be careful. If you use a combination that Quattro Pro already uses (for example, Ctrl+C for Copy), you will replace Quattro Pro's shortcut with your own. For a list of Ctrl+key combinations Quattro Pro uses, open the Help menu; then, select Contents, Essentials, Keyboard Techniques, and Special Keys.

Playing Back a Macro

To play back a macro, you must first open the notebook in which the macro is stored. (You can create a special macro notebook, as explained later, and keep it open and minimized on the desktop.) To run a macro, perform the following steps:

1. Make sure the notebook that contains the macro is open. You can run a macro stored in one notebook from another notebook, but the macro notebook must be open.

2. Open the Tools menu, select Macro, and select Play. The Play Macro dialog box appears, as shown in Figure 24.2, prompting you to select a macro.

Lesson 24

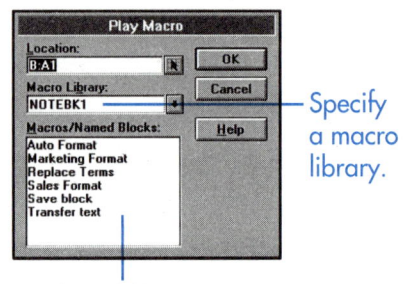

Figure 24.2 Select the macro you want to run.

(Specify a macro library. — List of macros in selected library)

3. In the Macro Library text box, do one of the following:

    - Select a macro library from the list.
    - Type the name of the open notebook that contains the macro commands. A list of the available macros appears.

4. Click on the macro you want to run.

5. Click on the OK button. Quattro Pro runs the selected macro.

> **Pressing a Shortcut Key** If you assigned the macro to a shortcut key combination, you can play the macro quickly by pressing the correct key combination.

Making a Macro Library

Storing macros in separate notebooks makes the macros difficult to use. A better way is to store all your macros in one notebook, creating a *macro library*, and leave the notebook open as you work. Whenever you enter the Tools, Macro, Play command, Quattro Pro then displays a list of the

Automating Your Work with Macros

macros in the macro library. To create a library, take the following steps:

1. Open the notebook you want to use as the macro library, or create a new notebook.

2. Create the macros you want to store in the library, and/or copy macros from other notebooks into this notebook.

3. Right-click inside the notebook's title bar and select Macro Library.

4. Click on Yes to use this notebook as a macro library, and then click on the OK button.

5. Use the File, Save command to save the notebook.

Once the notebook is saved, you can minimize the notebook window to keep it out of the way. When you want to play a macro, perform the steps described in the previous section. The new macro library will appear on the Macro Library drop-down list. Select the library to view the list of macros it contains.

> **Opening a Macro Library at Startup** To have the macro library available when you start Quattro Pro, right-click on the Quattro Pro title bar and select File Options. Type the drive and directory where the macro notebook is stored, tab to the Autoload File text box, and type the name of the macro notebook. Click on the OK button.

In this lesson, you learned how to record and play macros. The appendix that follows explains the basics of getting around in Windows and entering commands in Quattro Pro.

Appendix

Microsoft Windows Primer

In this appendix, you will learn the basics of using Microsoft Windows and entering commands in Quattro Pro.

Starting Microsoft Windows

To start Windows, do the following:

1. At the DOS prompt, type **win**.

2. Press Enter.

The Windows title screen appears for a few moments, and then you see a screen like the one in Figure A.1.

> **What If It Didn't Work?** You may have to change to the Windows directory before starting Windows; to do so, type **CD \WINDOWS** and press Enter.

Microsoft Windows Primer   147

Figure shows Windows Program Manager with labeled callouts: Pull-down menu, Control-menu box, Menu bar, Title bar, Minimize button, Maximize button, Scroll bar, Mouse pointer, Icons, Program groups, Program group window.

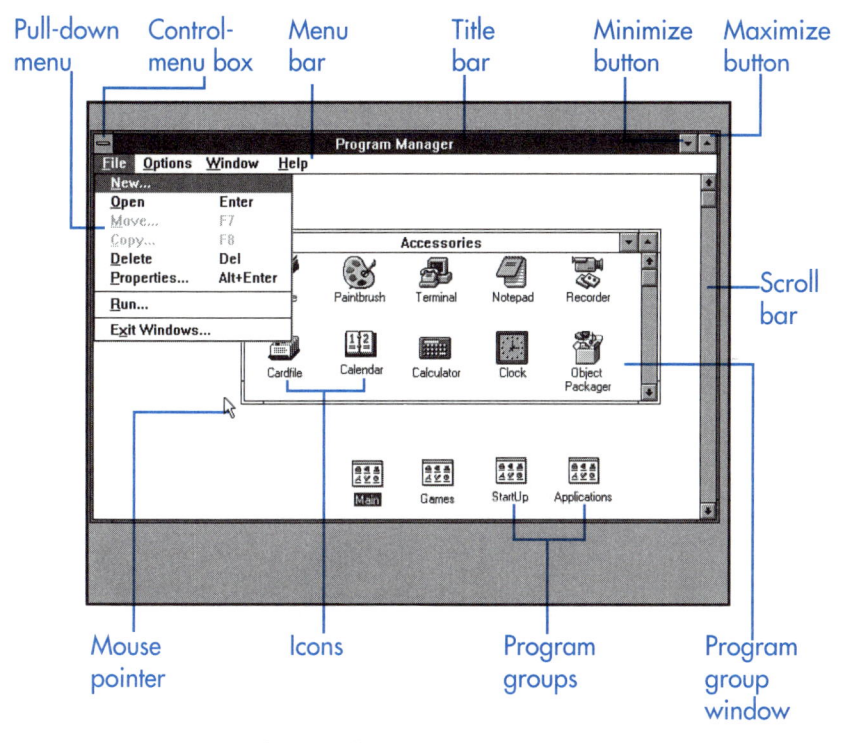

Figure A.1 The Windows Program Manager.

Parts of a Windows Screen

As shown in Figure A.1, the Windows screen contains several unique elements you won't see in DOS. Here's a brief summary.

Title bar Shows the name of the window or application.

Program group windows Contain program-item icons that allow you to run applications.

Icons Graphic representations of applications. To run an application, you select its icon.

Minimize and Maximize buttons   Alter a window's size. The Minimize button shrinks the window to the size of an icon. The Maximize button expands the window to fill the screen. When maximized, a window contains a double-headed arrow *Restore* button, which returns the window to its original size.

Control-menu box   When selected, pulls down a menu that offers size and location controls for the window. Double-click on this box to close the currently open window.

Pull-down menu bar   Contains a list of the pull-down menus available in the application.

Mouse pointer   If you are using a mouse, the mouse pointer (usually an arrow) appears on-screen. It can be controlled by moving the mouse (discussed later in this appendix).

Scroll bars   If a window contains more information than it can display, you will see a scroll bar. Clicking on the *scroll arrows* on each end of the scroll bar allows you to scroll slowly. Clicking on the *scroll box* allows you to scroll more quickly.

Using a Mouse

To work most efficiently in Windows, you should use a mouse. You can press mouse buttons and move the mouse in various ways to change the way it acts:

Point means to move the mouse pointer onto the specified item by moving the mouse. The tip of the mouse pointer must be touching the item.

Microsoft Windows Primer   149

Click on an item means to move the pointer onto the specified item and press the mouse button once. Unless specified otherwise, use the left mouse button.

Double-click on an item means to move the pointer onto the specified item and press and release the left mouse button twice quickly.

Drag means to move the mouse pointer onto the specified item, hold down the mouse button, and move the mouse while holding down the button.

Figure A.2 shows how to use the mouse to perform common Windows activities, including running applications and moving and resizing windows.

Click to control size and location.

Double-click to run an application.

Click to shrink.

Click to expand.

Drag title bar to move window.

Double-click to restore application.

Drag border to size window.

Double-click to restore the program group window.

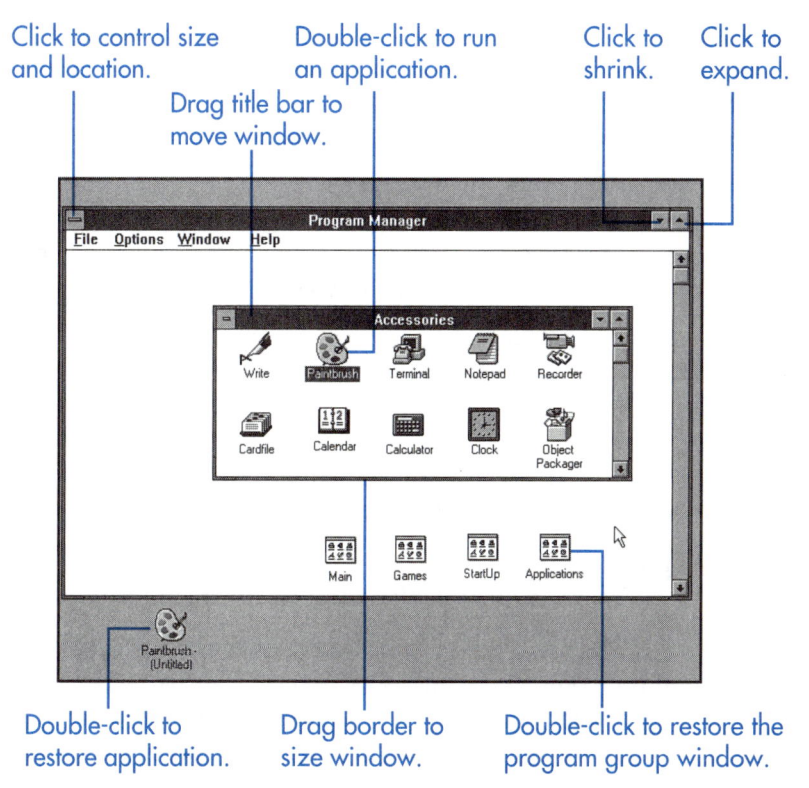

Figure A.2 Use your mouse to control Windows.

Starting an Application

To start an application, double-click on its icon. If its icon is contained in a program group window that's not open at the moment, open the window first. Follow these steps:

1. If necessary, open the program group window that contains the application you want to run. To open a program group window, double-click on its icon.

2. Double-click on the icon for the application you want to run.

Using Menus

The *menu bar* contains various pull-down menus (see Figure A.3) from which you can select commands. Each Windows application you run has a set of pull-down menus; Windows itself has a set too. To open a menu, click on its name on the menu bar. Once a menu is open, you can select a command from it by clicking on the desired command.

> **Shortcut Keys** Notice that in Figure A.3, some commands are followed by key names such as **Enter** (for the Open command) or **F8** (for the Copy command). These are called *shortcut keys*. You can use these keys to perform the commands without even opening the menu.

Usually, when you select a command, the command is performed immediately. However:

- If the command name is gray (instead of black), the command is unavailable at the moment, and you cannot choose it.

- If the command name is followed by an arrow, selecting the command will cause another menu to appear, from which you must select another command.

Microsoft Windows Primer

- If the command name is followed by an ellipsis (three dots), selecting it will cause a dialog box to appear. You'll learn about dialog boxes in the next section.

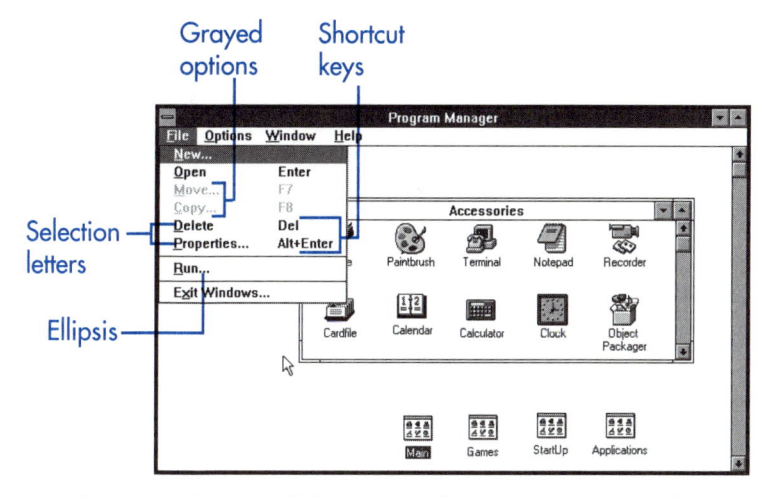

Figure A.3 A pull-down menu lists various commands you can perform.

Bypass Menus with the Toolbar In Quattro Pro, most menu commands have a corresponding button in the Toolbar. Instead of pulling down a menu and selecting a command, simply click on that command's button on the Toolbar.

Navigating Dialog Boxes

A dialog box is Windows' way of requesting additional information. For example, if you choose Print from the File menu of the Write application, you'll see the dialog box shown in Figure A.4.

Appendix

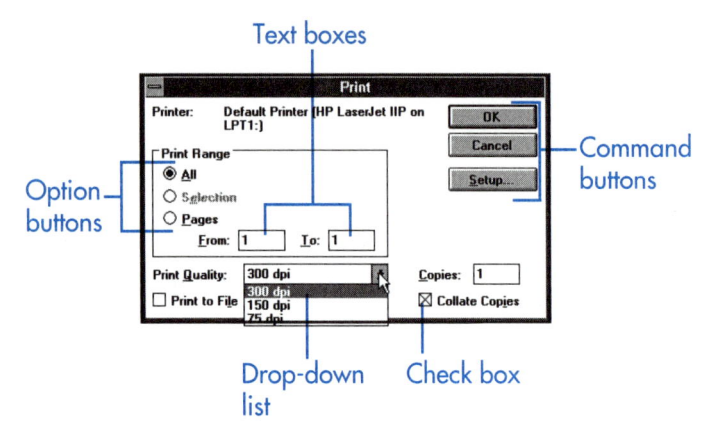

Figure A.4 A typical dialog box.

Each dialog box contains one or more of the following elements:

List boxes display available choices. To activate a list, click inside the list box. If the entire list is not visible, use the scroll bar to view the items in the list. To select an item from the list, click on it.

Drop-down lists are similar to list boxes, but only one item in the list is shown. To see the rest of the items, click on the down arrow to the right of the list box. To select an item from the list, click on it.

Text boxes allow you to type an entry. To activate a text box, click inside it. To edit an existing entry, use the arrow keys to move the cursor and the Del or Backspace keys to delete existing characters. Then type your correction.

Microsoft Windows Primer 153

Check boxes allow you to select one or more items in a group of options. For example, if you are styling text, you can select Bold and Italic to have the text appear in both bold and italic type. Click on a check box to activate it.

Option buttons are like check boxes, but you can select only one option button in a group. Selecting one button deselects any option that is already selected. Click on an option button to activate it.

Command buttons execute (or cancel) the command once you have made your selections in the dialog box. To press a command button, click on it.

Right-Clicking in Quattro Pro

In Quattro Pro, and some other Windows applications, you can enter commands by right-clicking on a selection or object. In Quattro Pro, right-clicking opens a dialog box called an *object inspector*. The following object inspectors are available:

Application: If you right-click inside the Quattro Pro title bar, you can enter default settings for how Quattro Pro operates.

Notebook: Right-click inside a notebook window title bar to change the default settings for only the selected notebook.

Page: Right-click inside a page tab to change the page properties, such as its name and color.

Block: Select a cell or cell block, and right-click on it to cut, copy, or delete the block; you can also right-click to format a selected block, or to perform other block operations.

Graph Window: Right-click on a graph window to control its aspect ratio and whether the graph displays grid lines.

Graph Setup and Background: Right-click on various graph objects to change their properties, including their color, typestyle, and position.

In this appendix, you learned the basics of using Microsoft Windows and entering commands in Quattro Pro.

Index

Symbols

#AND# (Logical AND) logical operator, 29
#NOT# (Logical NOT) logical operator, 29
#OR# (Logical OR) logical operator, 29
$ (dollar sign), absolute cell references, 22
* (asterisk) wildcard, 114
... (ellipsis) commands, 151
< (less than)
    conditional operator, 114
    logical operator, 29
<= (less than or equal to)
    conditional operator, 114
    logical operator, 29
<> (less than or greater than but not equal to) logical operator, 29, 114
= (equal to)
    conditional operator, 113
    logical operator, 29
> (greater than)
    conditional operator, 113
    logical operator, 29
>= (greater than or equal to)
    conditional operator, 114
    logical operator, 29
? (question mark) wildcard, 114
@ (function sign), 24
@ (function) button (input line), 27
~ (tilde) wildcard, 114
Ø key command, 118

A

absolute references (cells), 21-22
activating notebook page groups, 85
Active Block dialog box, 59
Active Block object inspector, 55, 62-63
    adjusting row height, 51
    displaying, 50
Active Notebook Object Inspector, 23
Active Page object inspector, 82-84
adding
    attributes to fonts, 58
    cell addresses to function arguments, 27
    columns, 24-25
    footers to spreadsheets, 72-73
    headers to spreadsheets, 72-73
    objects to graphs, 96-99
    records to databases, 109-110
    rows, 24-25
    values to function arguments, 27
Align list (Property Band), 59
Align Toolbar, 99
alignment
    labels, 15-16
    options, 59
    text, 58-60
amortization schedules, 125-127
Analysis Tool Expert dialog boxes, 122, 125

applications
- right-clicking commands, 153
- starting, 150

area graphs, 87
assigning key commands to macros, 143
asterisk (*) wildcard, 114
axis (graphs), 88, 90

B

Backspace key, 43
bar graphs, 87
Block Insert dialog box, 52
Block menu commands
- Copy, 47
- Move, 47
- Sort, 112

Block Names dialog box, 40, 143
Block Properties dialog box, 15
Block Sort dialog box, 112
borders
- Column borders, 7, 49
- printing, 80
- Row borders, 7, 49

Budget Expert, 119-121
budget spreadsheets, 119-121
Budget Tools, 119
building crosstab reports, 131
bullet charts
- creating, 100-102
- displaying, 104
- selecting, 104

bypassing
- Clipboard operations, 47
- menus, 151
- Spreadsheet Print dialog boxes, 76

C

cell blocks, *see* ranges
cells, 2, 8
- absolute references, 21-22
- addresses, 27
- Clipboard, 46
- contents, 42-44
- copying, 44-45
- drawing lines around/between, 61-63
- formatting, 65-66
- locking, 84
- moving, 44-45
- naming, 40
- overlapping in labels, 14
- pasting, 46-47
- range selection, 36-38
- relative references, 21
- right-clicking commands, 154
- selecting by name, 41
- shading, 63-64
- styles, 67
- text alignment, 58-60
- unlocking, 84

centering
- printouts, 80
- spreadsheet titles, 59

changing
- column widths, 48-50
- fonts, 57-58
- formula recalculation settings, 23
- notebook page settings, 83-84
- row height, 50-51
- styles, 69

changing cells (scenarios), 137
check boxes, 153
Clear command (Edit menu), 44
Clear Values command (Edit menu), 44
clicking (mouse), 149
clip art, 102
Clipboard, 46-47
Close command (File menu), 33
closing
- notebooks, 33
- spreadsheet panes, 10

Coaches (Help), 3
colors
- graphs, 90
- palettes, 64
- tabs, 84
- text, 58

columns
- adding, 24-25
- borders, 7, 49
- deleting, 52-53
- inserting, 51-52
- titles, 53-54
- widths, 48-50

command buttons, 153
commands
- ... (ellipsis), 151
- arrow prompts, 150
- Block menu, 47, 112
- dimmed commands, 150

Index

Edit menu
  Clear, 44
  Clear Values, 44
  Copy, 46
  Cut, 46
  Go To, 10, 41
  Paste, 47
  Paste Special, 47
  Redo, 43
File menu
  Close, 33
  Exit, 4
  Open, 33
  Page Setup, 70
  Print, 76, 99
  Print Preview, 77
  Print Scaling, 74
  Save, 31
  Save As, 32
Gadget menu, 133-134
Graphics menu
  Edit Graph, 93
  Graph Gallery, 101
Macro submenu, 141-143
Notebook menu
  Define Group, 85
  Define Style, 68
Preferences menu, 134
right-clicking, 153-154
Tools menu
  Data Modeling Desktop, 129
  Database Tools, 109, 114
  Group, 98
  Macro, 141
  Object Order, 98
  Scenario Manager, 139
View menu
  Group Mode, 85
  Locked Titles, 53
conditional operators (database searches), 113-114
Control-menu box, 148
Copy command
  Block menu, 47
  Edit menu, 46
Copy to Quattro Pro Options command (Preferences menu), 134
Copy to Quattro Pro Options dialog box, 134

copying
  cells, 44-46
  crosstab reports to notebooks, 134
  formulas, 21
  notebooks, 32-35
  ranges, 44-47
  records, 116
Create Report button, 138
Create Series dialog box, 16
Create Slide Show button, 102
creating
  amortization schedules, 125-127
  budget spreadsheets, 119-121
  bullet charts, 100-102
  crosstab reports, 129-130
  databases, 108-109
  graphs, 88-90
  macro libraries, 144-145
  refinance spreadsheets, 122-124
  scenarios, 136-138, 140
  slide shows, 100, 102-103
Criteria Table Point button, 117
criteria tables (record searches), 116
crosstab reports, 129-134
customizing
  graphs, 94-96
  slide shows, 104-105
  styles, 68-69
Cut command (Edit menu), 46
cutting cells in Clipboard, 46

D

data analysis, 128-134
data entry
  databases, 110
  spreadsheets, 12-17
Data Modeling Desktop Gadgets, 133-134
Data Modeling Desktop command (Tools menu), 129
Data Query dialog box, 117
data series (graphs), 88
Database Form dialog box, 109, 114
Database Tools command (Tools menu), 109, 114
databases, 108-118
date formats, 15
dates (spreadsheets), 14-15
defaults (printouts), 81

Define Group command (Notebook menu), 85
Define Style command (Notebook menu), 68
Define/Modify Group dialog box, 85
Define/Modify Style dialog box, 68
Delete key, 43
Delete Graph (Graphics menu option), 92
deleting
 cell contents, 44
 columns, 52-53
 formats, 67
 objects, 98
 rows, 52-53
Desktop labels, 131
dialog boxes
 navigating, 151-153
 see also individual dialog box names
 dimmed commands, 150
directory contents, 34
Display command (Gadget menu), 133
display sizes (notebooks), 83
displaying
 Active Block object inspector, 50
 bullet charts, 104
 graphs, 92-94
 grid lines, 63
 slide shows, 103, 105
 spreadsheet page settings, 70-71
 Toolbar button names, 3
 values in notebooks, 84
dollar sign ($), absolute cell references, 22
double-clicking (mouse), 149
Drag and Drop, 44-45
dragging, 149
 column borders, 49
 graph frames, 91
drawing lines around/between cells, 61-63
drilling entries in notebook page groups, 86
drop-down lists, 152

E

Edit Graph command (Graphics menu), 92-93
Edit keys, 42-43

Edit menu commands
 Clear, 44
 Clear Values, 44
 Copy, 46
 Cut, 46
 Go To, 10, 41
 Paste, 47
 Paste Special, 47
 Redo, 43
edit slide show window, 103
editing
 cell contents, 42-43
 graphs, 93
 income items (Budget Expert), 120
 scenarios, 139
 text, 12
ellipsis (...) commands, 151
End key, 43
enlarging page displays, 78
entering
 formulas in spreadsheets, 20
 functions, 25-27
 numbers as labels, 13
equal to (=)
 conditional operator, 113
 logical operator, 29
Exit command (File menu), 4
exiting
 Help, 4
 Print Preview window, 78
 Quattro Pro, 4
expanding highlighting capabilities, 38
Expense List (Budget Expert), 120
Experts dialog box, 89, 119

F

F1 key command, 3
F4 key command, 22
F5 key command, 10, 41
F7 key command, 38
F9 key command, 23
field names (databases), 108
fields
 searching, 116-118
 sorting, 112
File menu commands
 Close, 33
 Exit, 4
 Open, 33

Index **159**

Page Setup, 70
Print, 76, 99
Print Preview, 77
Print Scaling, 74
Save, 31
Save As, 32
files, *see* notebooks
financial spreadsheets, 119-127
Fit button (column widths), 48-49
flipping notebook pages, 8
fonts
  attributes, 58
  changing, 57-58
  crosstab reports, 134
footers, 72-73
Format command (Gadget menu), 133
formats
  date formats, 15
  numeric formats, 55
  removing, 67
  styles, 66-67
formatting
  cells, 65-66
  ranges, 65-66
  tables, 65-66
  values, 55-56
Formula command (Gadget menu), 133
Formula Composer utility, 25-27
Formula Expert dialog box, 26
formulas
  cell references, 21
  copying, 21
  entering in spreadsheets, 20
  Loan Life (Candidate), 124
  Loan Life (Current), 124
  printing, 80
  recalculation settings, 22-23
  spreadsheets, 18-19
  startup characters, 19
  Total Savings, 124
frames (graphs), 91
functions, 24-27

G

Gadgets (Data Modeling Desktop), 133-134
Go To command (Edit menu), 10, 41
Go To dialog box, 41
Graph Edit window, 94

Graph Expert, 88-90
Graph Gallery (Graphics menu option), 92, 101
Graph Gallery dialog box, 101
Graph Print dialog box, 99
Graph tool button, 90
Graph Toolbar, 93, 96-99
graphics, 102
Graphics menu commands, 91
  Edit Graph, 93
  Graph Gallery, 101
graphs, 88-99
greater than (>)
  conditional operator, 113
  logical operator, 29
greater than or equal to (>=)
  conditional operator, 114
  logical operator, 29
gridlines, 63, 80
Group command (Tools menu), 98
Group Mode command (View menu), 85
grouping notebook pages, 84-86

H

handles (graphs), 90
Header/Footer text boxes (Page Setup dialog box), 72
headers (spreadsheets), 72-73
headings, 80
heirarchy (operators), 19-20
Help, 2-4
hiding grid lines, 63
high-low graphs, 87
highlighting expansion, 38
home financing, 119-127
Home key, 43

I

icons, 147
importing graphics, 102
income items (Budget Expert), 120
input line, 5, 12, 27
Insert mode (spreadsheets), 13
inserting, 51-52
  graphs, 90

J–K

jumps, 4
key commands
   Ø, 118
   assigning to macros, 143
   Backspace key, 43
   Delete key, 43
   Edit keys, 42-43
   End key, 43
   F1, 3
   F4, 22
   F5, 10, 41
   F7, 38
   F9, 23
   Home key, 43
   spreadsheet navigation, 8-10

L

label bars (crosstab reports), 132
labels
   alignment, 15-16
   crosstab reports, 131
   Desktop, 131
   overlapping cells, 14
   spreadsheets, 11-12
layering graph objects, 98-99
legends (graphs), 88
less than (<)
   conditional operator, 114
   logical operator, 29
less than or equal to (<=)
   conditional operator, 114
   logical operator, 29
less than or greater than but not equal to (<>) logical operator, 29
Limit command (Gadget menu), 133
line graphs, 87
lines (cells), 61-63
list boxes, 152
listing
   alignment options, 59
   numeric formats, 55
lists
   bulleted lists, 101-102
   Expense List (Budget Expert), 120
   Income List (Budget Expert), 120
Loan Life (Candidate) formula, 124
Loan Life (Current) formula, 124
loans
   amortization schedules, 125-127
   refinancing, 122-124
Locked Titles command (View menu), 53
Locked Titles dialog box, 53
locking
   cells, 84
   column titles, 53-54
   row titles, 53-54
Logical AND (#AND#) logical operator, 29
Logical NOT (#NOT#) logical operator, 29
logical operators, 27-29
Logical OR (#OR#) logical operator, 29

M

Macro command (Tools menu), 141
macro libraries, 145
Macro submenu commands, 141-143
macros, 141-145
margins (spreadsheets), 73-74
Maximize button, 117, 148
menu bar, 5
menus
   bypassing, 151
   Graphics menu, 91
   navigating, 150-151
   opening, 150
Minimize button (Data Query title bar), 148
modifying graphs, 91-92
mouse, 148-149
Move command (Block menu), 47
moving
   cells, 44-45
   graphs, 90-91
   objects, 98
   ranges, 44-45, 47
   Selector, 8

N

Name command (Gadget menu), 134
naming
   axis (graphs), 90
   cells, 40
   macros, 143
   notebooks, 30

Index

page groups, 85-86
pages, 82-83
ranges, 40
scenarios, 137
slide shows, 102, 104
navigating
   dialog boxes, 151-153
   menus, 150-151
   mouse, 148-149
   notebooks
      pages, 8
      windows, 6-10
   Quattro Pro window, 5-6
   spreadsheet pages, 8-10
not equal to (<>) conditional operator, 114
Notebook menu commands
   Define Group, 85
   Define Style, 68
notebooks, 2
   closing, 33
   copying, 32-35
   copying crosstab reports, 134
   display sizes, 83
   naming, 30
   opening, 33-34
   page groups, 85-86
   pages, 82
      changing settings, 83-84
      flipping, 8
      grouping, 84-86
      naming, 82-83
      ungrouping, 85
   passwords, 32
   right-clicking commands, 153
   saving, 30-32
   Scenarios report page, 138
   values, 84
   windows, 6-10
   zooming, 83
numbers (labels), 13
numeric formats, 55

O

object inspectors, 95
Object Order command (Tools menu), 98
objects
   Active Block object inspector, 50
   adding to graphs, 96-99
   deleting, 98
   graphs, 94-96

Help, 3
layering, 98-99
moving, 98
selecting, 97-98
sizing, 98
Open command (File menu), 33
Open File dialog box, 33
opening
   macro libraries at startup, 145
   menus, 150
   notebooks, 33-34
operators
   conditional operators (database searches), 113-114
   heirarchy, 19-20
   logical operators, 27-29
option buttons, 79, 153
options
   Graphics menu, 91
   printing, 79-81
orientation (printers), 71-72
Output Block Point button, 117
Overtype mode (spreadsheets), 13

P

page displays, 78
page groups, 85-86
Page Name text box, 82
Page Setup command (File menu), 70
page setup settings (spreadsheets), 75
pages (notebooks)
   grouping, 84-86
   right-clicking commands, 153
   ungrouping, 85
Palette Toolbar, 99
palettes, 64
Pane splitter, 7
paper types (printers), 71
passwords (notebooks), 32
Paste button (Toolbar), 47
Paste command (Edit menu), 47
Paste Special command (Edit menu), 47
pasting cells, 46-47
pie graphs, 87
Play command (Macro submenu), 143
Play Macro dialog box, 143
playing back macros, 143-144
Point button (dialog boxes), 39
Polygon tools, 97
Polyline tools, 97

Preferences menu commands, 134
previewing spreadsheet printouts, 77-79
Print button, 79
Print command (File menu), 76, 99
Print Preview command (File menu), 77
Print Preview window, 78
Print Scaling command (File menu), 74
printers, 71-72
printing
　borders, 80
　formulas, 80
　graphs, 99
　gridlines, 80
　options, 79-81
　ranges, 76-77
　slide shows, 105-106
printouts
　centering, 80
　defaults, 81
program group windows, 1, 147
Properties option (graph objects), 95
Property Band, 5
　Align list, 59
　Property list, 96
　Style list, 67
　Zoom Factor, 83
Property list (Property Band), 96
Pull-down menu bar, 148

Q

Quattro Pro
　quitting, 4
　starting, 1-2
　window, 5-6
question mark (?) wildcard, 114
quitting
　Help, 4
　Print Preview window, 78
　Quattro Pro, 4

R

ranges
　copying, 44-45, 47
　cutting/copying to Clipboard, 46
　formatting, 65-66
　inserting, 51-52
　moving, 44-45, 47
　naming, 40
　printing, 76-77
　right-clicking commands, 154
　selecting, 36-39
　shading, 63-64
　specifying in dialog boxes, 38-39
　styles, 67
　typing, 38-39
rearranging crosstab report data, 132
recalculation settings (formulas), 22-23
Record command (Macro sub-menu), 141
Record Macro dialog box, 141
recording macros, 141-143
records
　adding to databases, 108-110
　copying, 116
　database search forms, 114-115
　searching, 113-118
　sorting, 111
Redo command (Edit menu), 43
reducing page displays, 78
refinance spreadsheets, 122-124
Refinance tool, 122-124
refinancing loans, 122-124
relative references (cells), 21
removing
　formats, 67
　label bars from crosstab reports, 132
repeating headings, 80
reports, *see* crosstab reports
resizing graphs, 90-91
right-clicking commands, 153-154
Row borders, 7
rows
　adding, 24-25
　deleting, 52-53
　height, 50-51
　inserting, 51-52
　titles, 53-54
Run Slide Show button (Toolbar), 103

S

Save As command (File menu), 32
Save command (File menu), 31
Save File dialog box, 31
saving
　databases, 110
　notebooks, 30-32
　page setup settings (spreadsheets), 75

Index

scaling spreadsheets, 74-75
Scenario Expert, 136-138
Scenario Expert dialog boxes, 137
Scenario Manager, 138
Scenario Manager command (Tools menu), 139
Scenario Manager dialog box, 139
Scenario Reports, 140
scenarios, 135-140
Scenarios report page (notebooks), 138
screens, 147-148
scroll bars, 7, 148
Search Records form, 115
searching
　fields, 116-118
　records, 113-118
Select-All button, 7
Selected Objects object inspector, 104
selecting
　Budget Tools, 119
　bullet charts, 104
　cells by name, 41
　changing cells (scenarios), 137
　fonts, 57-58
　functions, 27
　numeric formats, 55
　objects, 97-98
　printers
　　orientation, 71-72
　　paper types, 71-72
　printing options, 79-81
　ranges, 36-39
　spreadsheet page cells, 7
　styles, 67
Selector, 7-8
Send Data to Data Modeling Desktop dialog box, 129
Series (Graphics menu option), 92
Setup button, 79
shading
　cells, 63-64
　ranges, 63-64
shortcut keys, 150
　see also key commands
sizing
　graphs, 90-91
　objects, 98
Slide Show Expert, 103-104
Slide Show Expert dialog boxes, 104
slide shows, 100-106
Sort command (Block menu), 112
sorting, 111-113

SpeedFill dialog box, 16
SpeedFill utility, 16-17
SpeedFormat dialog box, 66
SpeedFormat utility, 65-66
SpeedSum utility, 24-25
SpeedTab button, 7
spell-checker, 43
splitting
　notebook windows, 7
　spreadsheet pages, 10
Spreadsheet Page Setup dialog box, 70
Spreadsheet Print dialog box, 77
Spreadsheet Print Options dialog box, 79
spreadsheets
　budget spreadsheets, 119-121
　data entry, 12-17
　dates, 14-15
　financial spreadsheets, 119-127
　footers, 72-73
　formulas, 18-19
　　copying, 21
　　entering, 20
　　recalculation settings, 22-23
　functions, 24
　headers, 72-73
　Insert mode, 13
　labels, 11-12
　margins, 73-74
　notebooks, 30-32
　Overtype mode, 13
　page displays, 78
　pages
　　navigating, 8-10
　　selecting cells, 7
　　settings, 70-71
　　splitting, 10
　　viewing, 7
　printouts, 77-79
　refinance spreadsheets, 122-124
　scaling, 74-75
　scenarios, 135-136
　split pages, 10
　split windows, 10
　titles, 59
　values, 11-12
starting
　applications, 150
　Quattro Pro, 1-2
　Windows, 146-147
startup characters (formulas), 19
Status line, 6
Stop Record command (Macro submenu), 142

storing macros, 144-145
Style list (Property Band), 67
styles, 66-69
styles (text), 57
switching between spreadsheet panes, 10

T

tab scrolls, 7
tables
    criteria tables, 116
    formatting, 65-66
tabs, 6, 84
text, 12, 57-60
text boxes, 152
tilde (~) wildcard, 114
title bar, 147
titles (graphs), 90
Titles (Graphics menu option), 92
Toolbar, 3, 5
    command buttons, 151
    font attribute buttons, 58
    Paste button, 47
    Run Slide Show button, 103
toolbars
    Align Toolbar, 99
    Graph Toolbar, 93, 96-99
    Palette Toolbar, 99
tools
    Polygon tools, 97
    Polyline tools, 97
    Refinance tool, 122-124
Tools menu
    Data Modeling Desktop, 129
    Database Tools, 109, 114
    Group, 98
    Macro, 141
    Object Order, 98
    Scenario Manager, 139
    Spell Check, 43
Total Savings formula, 124
Type (Graphics menu option), 92
typing ranges, 38-39

U

undoing
    cell content changes, 43-44
    formats, 67

ungrouping notebook pages, 85
unlocking
    cells, 84
    column titles, 54
    row titles, 54
updating Scenario Reports, 140
utilities
    Formula Composer, 25-27
    SpeedFill, 16-17
    SpeedSum, 24-25

V

values
    adding to function arguments, 27
    displaying in notebooks, 84
    formatting, 55-56
    scenarios, 135-136
    spreadsheets, 11-12
View Graph (Graphics menu option), 92
View menu commands
    Group Mode, 85
    Locked Titles, 53
viewing
    directory contents, 34
    scenarios, 137, 139
    spreadsheet pages, 7

W

wildcards, 114
Windows
    screen, 147-148
    starting, 146-147
windows
    edit slide show window, 103
    Graph Edit window, 94
    notebook windows, 6-10
    Print Preview window, 78
    program group window, 1
    program group windows, 147
    Quattro Pro window, 5-6

Z

Zoom Factor (Property Band), 83
Zoom in button, 78
Zoom out button, 78
zooming
    notebooks, 83
    page displays, 78